"'Adaptive' is the operative word—change or fail. This is leadership through empowering and training others to succeed in a rapidly changing environment and is a must-read for all disciplines—HR, finance, marketing, operations, and engineering, in addition to sales. It is servant leadership. As he does in his life, Lee brings this compelling, enlightening, and inspirational work with integrity and energy."

—Jim Balkcom

civilian aide to SECARMY

"In Winning Adaptive Sales, *Lee Hicks inspires us with his story and energizes leading salespeople to navigate the quickly changing landscape of sales to increasingly complex businesses. He leverages his vast experience and strengths in this book to translate an easy-to-follow winning sales methodology. Every executive, and certainly every sales manager and person, should put this book on their 'must-read' list for success in business and life."*

—Dominic C. Mazzone

managing director, Mazzone & Associates

"Lee Hicks is the real deal—a great person, a dynamic leader, a nationally acclaimed speaker, and now a great author. He has written one of the best books on the disciplines of adaptive selling that I have ever read—and I have read them all. Having sold over $1 billion in consumer products, I know what it takes to be successful in sales. If you read and apply the simple principals that Lee outlines in his book, it will help make you a better sales professional and, more importantly, a better person. I highly recommend you read this book if you want to take your selling (and life) skills to the next level."

—Steven Cesari

president, the Cesari Companies; best-selling author, *Clarity: How to Get It, How to Keep It & How to Use It to Balance Your Life*

"Lee's Adaptive Sales techniques have been a guiding light for me in most every endeavor I have engaged in since he taught me its key principles. I have found them instrumental in negotiating international mergers and acquisitions as an executive for Fortune 500 company Equifax Inc., helping to establish and grow the Georgia Restaurant Association, and building the successful cybersecurity company PCI University. I am delighted that Lee is now sharing his innovative sales methodologies, winning formulas for success, and personal-value-based life philosophies in the form of a much-awaited book."

—Charles Y. Hoff, JD, MBA

Law Offices of Charles Y. Hoff, PC

"Searching for and developing high-quality salespeople is an ongoing challenge everywhere. I welcome Lee's book, which emphasizes the 'others-focused' approach to effective selling. Focusing on the needs of others is a core part of what we teach at Birkman when it comes to developing insightful leaders across the board. Whether they lead or sell in companies, churches, or nonprofits, Lee's wisdom will apply."

—Sharon Birkman Fink

CEO, Birkman International, Inc.

"Lee Hicks is waking up the sales world! Whether you like it or not, your buyer has changed forever. That buyer is arming himself or herself with information online, through social networks and other digital means, to make informed decisions. This is happening without you, unless you adapt quickly."

—Jamie Shanks

CEO, Sales for Life

"In the time frame I have had the privilege and pleasure of knowing and working on specific projects with Lee, I can certainly attest that he lives his personal life as he lives his professional life. His commitment, integrity, and passion in what and how he lives are well captured in this book. His thoughts are simple and direct and can allow any person to implement his thoughts, principles, and techniques to positively impact their personal and professional life. T-R-U-S-T is the foundation!"

—Gustavo Arenas

SVP & chief sales officer (retired), AMD (Advanced Micro Devices); president, Escuderia TelMex USA

"One of life's greatest achievements is finding out what you want to do with your life, doing it, and inspiring others with what you have learned. Lee Hicks does just that by sharing his passion and life's work in very straight-forward fashion in Winning Adaptive Sales.*"*

—Mike Potts

integration executive, CISCO; previous president & CEO, Lancope (now CISCO)

"Where does today's salesperson fit into a world where 75 percent of B-2-B decision makers say it's easier to buy from a website than from a salesperson? How does one avoid becoming a DSR (Dying Sales Rep) in today's evolving workplace? Check out this practical yet compelling resource for learning how to not only survive but THRIVE in the world of complex sales."

—Peyton Day

CEO, Roam Innovative Workplace

WINNING

ADAPTIVE SALES

WINNING

A D A P T I V E   S A L E S

Accelerate Your Success by
**LEADING WITH
INSIGHTS**

LEE HICKS

Published by Advantage, Charleston, South Carolina.
Member of Advantage Media Group.

ADVANTAGE is a registered trademark, and the Advantage colophon is a trademark of Advantage Media Group, Inc.

Printed in the United States of America.

ISBN: 978-1-59932-774-7
LCCN: 2016948658

Cover design by George Stevens.

This publication is designed to provide accurate and authoritative information in regard to the subject matter covered. It is sold with the understanding that the publisher is not engaged in rendering legal, accounting, or other professional services. If legal advice or other expert assistance is required, the services of a competent professional person should be sought.

Advantage Media Group is proud to be a part of the Tree Neutral® program. Tree Neutral offsets the number of trees consumed in the production and printing of this book by taking proactive steps such as planting trees in direct proportion to the number of trees used to print books. To learn more about Tree Neutral, please visit **www.treeneutral.com.**

Advantage Media Group is a publisher of business, self-improvement, and professional development books. We help entrepreneurs, business leaders, and professionals share their Stories, Passion, and Knowledge to help others Learn & Grow. Do you have a manuscript or book idea that you would like us to consider for publishing? Please visit **advantagefamily.com** or call **1.866.775.1696.**

To Fredda, for believing in me, challenging me, encouraging me, and loving me unconditionally. To Bentley-Grace and Henry: always dream big, work hard, give more than you take, serve others first, and love the Lord with all your heart!

CONTENTS

FOREWORD

As the founding Chief Marketing Officer of Web MD and the founder of Vitrue, which was acquired by Oracle, where I am now senior vice president of product development, I know what it means to build a winning team. My story has been well documented over the years, so it's no surprise that my road to success hasn't been one, consistent upward trajectory—nor has it been a solo venture. Along the way, I've had great friends, mentors, and coaches who have helped guide my steps. That's one of the keys to succeeding in life: knowing when to have faith in the knowledge that others bring to the game.

In fact, one of the greatest lessons in my career was learning that what's truly significant in life is the impact that you make on others—and that they can make on you.

Since our first meeting, I've seen the impact Lee Hicks has made on others.

Like many successful leaders, he has overcome many obstacles in both his personal and professional life. And like me, Lee's life has been strongly influenced by his relationship with God. He understands that to truly win, we need God on our side for He is the true Head Coach.

This book, *Winning Adaptive Sales: Accelerate Your Success by Leading with Insights*, shares Lee's insights for getting ahead in sales—and ultimately in life.

One of my favorite Bible passages is Philippians 2:3–4, which says, "Do nothing out of selfish ambition or vain conceit, but in humility consider others better than yourselves. Each of you should look not only to your own interests, but also to the interests of others." That's what is at the core of Lee's Adaptive Sales program. As a longtime sales professional, Lee understands that what really matters in sales goes beyond products and services—it's about meeting needs for the greater good. *Winning Adaptive Sales* will help you develop your insights and use your talents and inner strength to make the world a better place. Because it takes inner strength and courage to win in sales, and in the game of life.

—Reggie Bradford

ACKNOWLEDGMENTS

Thanks to the army of people who have made this book possible. To Sheila Henry, my high school English literature teacher, who helped me see the growth that comes from a love of reading, and to Coach T. McFerrin, my football coach and history teacher, who helped me appreciate history as a guide to the future and also developed in me a deep appreciation for mastering fundamentals to achieve a competitive advantage, both on and off the field.

Thanks also to those who helped shaped me during my impressionable college years at the University of Georgia: the fraternity of Phi Gamma Delta, for teaching me that nothing can take the place of persistence and blessing me with an extended family of brothers; Coach Mike Castronis, my cheerleading coach, who showed me what "great" looks and acts like, especially in his final days battling cancer (I miss you, Coach Mike!); and Bill Bracewell, my sounding board, mentor, and advisor—essentially my "second father"—who made sure I didn't steer too far off course while navigating college's uncharted waters!

My thanks to Doug Mauldin, my boss at the Tilly Mill Gulf gas station where I worked during high school and college, who to this day doesn't know I overheard him tell one of his best customers that I would be rich some day because of my work ethic. His belief in me set the wheels of my career in motion.

To Dan McKee, my first sales manager at Control Data Corporation, for taking a chance on a kid with no sales experience but with a huge heart for learning, and for being part of a great team of role models like Steve Hicks, Richard Howe, Tom Brassell, David Barron, Sharon Randolph, Donna Croft, Steve Clay, Bart Biesecker, and Cathy Brandeis.

To Jerry Leonard at Dun & Bradstreet Software. His job offer to join the elite sales team—assembled by John Imlay, Rick Page, Brad Childress, and Curt Brassfield—that included Tom Noonan, Bill Zehmer, Dave Ward, Mike Zebleski, and so many other sales hall of famers put me in a league everyone dreams about but few get to experience. I didn't deserve it, but I am forever grateful!

To David Stargel and Peter Dunning, for bringing me into SAP in 1994 when the US market was unsure what R/2 and R/3 were. You showed me the future of enterprise software and what being a part of "hockey-stick growth" felt like. Once you've had it, you are always striving for it and are amazed and thankful when you experience it!

To Mike Potts and Giddy Hollander for giving me my first taste of executive leadership and early-stage technology start-up acceleration, teaching me the ropes of raising venture capital, and trusting me to build a team to drive the revenue to take Jacada public.

To Rick Page, now in heaven with our "Million Dollar Baby's" brother Lanier. You taught me what it means to be an authentic, "others focused," Winning the Complex Sales specialist and how to coach organizations and individuals to raise their game while leading their customers to do the same.

To Mike Dunn at PolyVision, a Steelcase Company, for trusting me to guide a hundred-year-old furniture manufacturer through the turbulent waters of incorporating Advanced Collaboration Technologies.

To Steve Hufford at Raymond James, for your friendship and counsel over the years and for sticking with me, and for continuing to stick with me even after you fired me (twice)—a story for another day! And to my other founders at C PORT Solutions, which grew into a leader in the unified collaboration and telemedicine market and was then successfully sold to Newell Rubbermaid to become the Rubbermaid Telemedicine Solutions business unit based on the energy, experience, and ethics of Larry Sanders, Michael Edmeades, Peter Muller, Jim Custer, Ray Johnson, Pap Datta, David Kassens, Pete McClain, Jackson Houk, Chuck Trippe, and Buddy Blaha.

To Pat Longworth at Kodiak Group, for your friendship and teamwork on growing a thriving sales and marketing consulting firm that continues to make a difference for global brands like Joe Gibbs Racing, Groupo Carso, Time Warner Cable (now Charter), ARRIS, and many others.

To Steve Gertz, for using Whitefield Academy's "Donuts with Dads" event as the instrument to connect me with Coach Joe Gibbs and Carlos Slim.

To my newest friends and partners in this journey of *Winning Adaptive Sales*: my amazing publishing team at Advantage Media Group, including Alison Morse, Claire Watson, Eland Mann, George Stevens, Regina Roths, Kirby Andersen, and Adam Witty; the entire team at Michaels Wilder, my amazing digital-marketing agency that has the undeniable talent to make even this guy look state-of-the-art;

and to Steve Nagle, Curtis Shaw, Mike Ryan, and Shelly Anderson, for your unwavering support, guidance, and insight on how "digital" should look, act, and feel to the market. To DigiVid360, the most talented video group in all of the United States. And to Andrew Chaifetz, the technology visionary that powers the Adaptive Sales University platform, enabling us to teach sales in a way that keeps us worlds apart from all of academia!

To Robert Consoli at Liaison Technologies. You were the "difference maker" on my sales team at Jacada. You touched my heart and became my best friend and accountability partner based on your sincere and deep personal relationship with Jesus Christ. My marriage, family life, and career are on solid ground because of your servant leadership in my life.

To Mom and Dad, for loving me, equipping me, guiding me, and encouraging me to live a "Yes You Can" life.

Finally, and most importantly, to my Lord and Savior Jesus Christ, for blessing this rusted piece of steel you named Lee Hicks with such an amazing network of your soldiers that proves to me there is a God, filled with grace, ready to pour it out to everyone who believes!

ABOUT THE AUTHOR

Lee Hicks is an entrepreneur, executive, sales leader, mentor, coach, and public speaker with over twenty-nine years' experience in leading early- and late-stage companies in their selling, coaching, and winning in the complex-sales environment. Lee is the founder and CEO of Winning Adaptive Sales, an H2 Strategies company. Winning Adaptive Sales is a "leadership fraternity" of the most successful people and technologies behind the sales industry's newest paradigm of sales methodology and enablement solutions.

Winning Adaptive Sales is Lee's second entrepreneurial endeavor, the first being C PORT Solutions, a unified collaboration and healthcare IT company that was sold to Newell Rubbermaid, which became Rubbermaid Telemedicine Solutions.

Lee's companies have been utilized by some of the world's most recognizable brands including Newell Rubbermaid, Time Warner Cable, Joe Gibbs Racing, SAP, Polycom, Groupo Carso, Toshiba, and many others.

Since entering the sales and marketing consulting world in 2001, Lee and his company, Winning Adaptive Sales, have trained and coached over fifteen thousand sales professionals who have sold over $15 billion in total contract revenue.

As an executive, sales professional, consultant, leader, and coach, Lee personally touches the heart of every team member, client, and launch event attendee, driving them to a new level of both personal and professional accomplishment.

Lee has a finance degree from the University of Georgia and has been a part of great organizations including Ceridian, Dun & Bradstreet Software, SAP, Steelcase, The Complex Sale, DSG Consulting, C PORT Solutions (a Newell Rubbermaid Company), and Kodiak Group. He is married to his amazing wife, Fredda, and they have two children, Bentley-Grace and Henry.

INTRODUCTION

When I sat down and began creating a plan to put this book together, I quickly realized how blessed my life has been. Sitting there, listing out all the thoughts I wanted to share and thinking about all the people I'd been involved with over the years—business associates, partners, friends—I began to see how much of an impact everyone has had on me.

Prior to becoming a sales consultant, I was in complex sales and leadership for eighteen years. Complex sales are large-contract transactions that typically involve multiple buyers with diverse expectations, multiple seller participants and competitors, strategic change initiatives, and multifaceted solutions.

During my time in complex sales, I was part of great organizations including Control Data Corporation (now Ceridian), Dun & Bradstreet Software, SAP, Steelcase, The Complex Sale, and DSG Consulting. Then I formed my own company, C PORT Solutions, which became a Newell Rubbermaid Company. In addition to Winning Adaptive Sales, I still engage as a consultant with Little Rock-based Kodiak Group.

Since launching my consulting career fifteen years ago in 2001, I've had the pleasure of leading and coaching over fifteen thousand complex-sales professionals around the world, ultimately driving over $15 billion of contract value, an accomplishment I summarize as "15 for 15 for 15."

This book is my opportunity to give back in return for all that's been given me by a comprehensive list of people whom I've named in the acknowledgments section. These are people who have been alongside me on this journey, helping me to form my insights and ultimately my voice. It's a journey that has allowed me to share my passion for serving, leading, and coaching others so that they can have the kind of career that I have been blessed with.

WINNING, RELEVANT SELLING TODAY

The Internet has obliterated the profession of sales, and I want to help you—today's sales leaders—take back control. With this book, I want to not only acknowledge the important place of sales representatives and leaders in our industry but also to suggest a new terminology for this more traditional designation: Adaptive Sales Professionals (ASPs). I want to place the spotlight of experience that I have amassed over the past twenty-nine years on you and your sales efforts to help propel you to be in the top 1 percent of the sales profession (what I call the *Trident Carriers*, a name I'll explain later)—not just now, but forever. I want you to feel the benefit of seeing a 30 percent improvement in sales productivity sixty days after you've been exposed to the Winning Adaptive Sales techniques and tools as provided at Adaptive Sales University. I want to see you promoted to an executive-level sales position twice as fast as you would have been without my coaching.

I also want to position sales as a commitment to leadership, because leadership is not simply for managers or executives—it is also for sales professionals who need to influence managers, executives, and key influencers with varying responsibilities. That's why it's crucial for ASPs to embrace leadership development to become more effective and relevant.

H2 Strategies and Adaptive Sales University provide the leadership skills, consulting, and coaching solutions to help ASPs develop the business acumen and sales strategic literacy for their esteemed profession. Yes, sales is an esteemed profession. No sales means no business. Sales requires insight, intellect, courage, creativity, tencacity, persuasiveness, persistence, and an ability to discern the other party's needs and meet them. That's called leadership. Servant leadership.

So, you may be asking yourself: What makes Winning Adaptive Sales unique among all of the sales and marketing methodologies out there today? It all boils down to **T-R-U-S-T:**

> ➤ **T**hought leadership
> ➤ **R**elationships at all levels
> ➤ **U**nderstanding the client's critical business objectives (CBOs)
> ➤ **S**trategic solutions that synergize with clients' CBOs
> ➤ **T**eam transparency

I'm also an internationally recognized leadership and sales expert—my "Lee Talks" have inspired thousands of leaders and sales professionals around the world. In these talks, I motivate people through real-life examples, humorous anecdotes, and time-tested principles. Some of my most popular speeches (which I'll talk about in the pages ahead) include:

> ➤ How to live a "Yes You Can" life

- ➤ What does being a trusted advisor demand?
- ➤ How to be sincerely "others focused"
- ➤ "IBAR: The pathway to great results"
- ➤ Transforming demand-reacting Dying Sales Reps (DSRs) into demand-creating ASPs

My organization, Winning Adaptive Sales, is geared toward enabling sales professionals to raise their game and become a positive force for others at work, at home, and in the community.

WHAT DRIVES ME

What drives me, in part, is an event that happened on April 17, 2001. That day set me on a course that I would not willingly have chosen but which would ultimately make me a better man—a better husband, a better father, a better professional, and a devoted philanthropist. It changed me forever.

That day, my wife, Fredda, was only twenty-one weeks pregnant with our twins, Lanier and Bentley-Grace, when she went into labor. Unfortunately, our son Lanier died and had to be delivered. But by God's great grace, Bentley-Grace survived and was able to be born three-and-one-half weeks later, allowing her just enough time to develop lung buds large enough to survive. On May 7, 2001, Bentley-Grace Hicks was born four months premature at one pound, six ounces.

The doctors painted a very bleak picture for our "preemie"—she wouldn't survive, they said, or if she did, she would never walk, talk, or see. She would never breathe without oxygen, eat without feeding tubes . . . well, you get the picture.

Happily, the doctors were wrong! Not only did Bentley-Grace live, but she can talk, she can breathe without supplemental oxygen, and she can eat without a feeding tube. The only thing they were right about was that she can't walk—yet! Just ask her and she will tell you that she will not just walk one day, but she will run!

Diagnosed with spastic quadriplegia cerebral palsy, Bentley-Grace is in a wheelchair and requires physical assistance around the clock. While BG, as she's lovingly known, may be physically disabled, she is all there mentally, emotionally, and spiritually. She is whole and holy to us and to countless others.

Today, BG is the reason for Team Bentley-Grace (check them out on Facebook), a group of people who rally in support of our beloved BG and disabled athletes everywhere. Team Bentley-Grace is a team that BG organized and manages on her own. BG's first competitive race was at the fortieth running of the Marine Corps Marathon in Washington, DC, where her team placed third out of sixty-five teams. The idea for Team BG was inspired by Team Hoyt (www.teamhoyt.com), the incredible father/son team competing in marathons nationwide—watching Dick wheeling his son Rick across a finish line is a "bucket-list" event!

Dick became my mentor in all aspects of life, inspiring me with the simple phrase "Yes You Can," which he inscribed on my copy of his book, *It's Only a Mountain*. Today, I'm on the board of directors for Disabled Sports USA (www.disabledsportsusa.org), an organization providing national leadership and opportunities for individuals with disabilities to develop independence, confidence, and fitness through participation in community sports, recreation, and educational programs.

A NEW PLATFORM

As I mentioned earlier, to help ASPs have the training and coaching value that's desperately needed today, I've created an affordable platform—Adaptive Sales University—which can be accessed from my corporate website, WinningAdaptiveSales.com. The Adaptive Sales University platform is a way for sales professionals to invest in sustainable skill development, leadership, and subject-matter literacy, which will produce an exponential return on investment for both themselves and their customers. Adaptive Sales University is a one-of-a-kind social-learning platform—imagine the power of Facebook meets the power of LinkedIn meets the power of Khan Academy meets the power of SlideShare.

If you are wondering where to take your organization, team, and career next, Winning Adaptive Sales and Adaptive Sales University will help you do the following:

Connect. At Winning Adaptive Sales, we serve individuals, corporations, institutions, civic associations, and organizations through one-on-one, small team, and large group sessions. In each of these sessions, we brainstorm innovation, assess challenges, engineer growth, focus on execution, coach performance, and inspire servant leadership—all in an effort to create a competitive advantage.

Equip. Discover, master, and execute the latest best practices as an ASP and, equally important, as a leader. By leveraging decades of complex-sales experience, research, and partnerships, Winning Adaptive Sales and Adaptive Sales University serve its members and partners by focusing on the issues that are most relevant and impactful to their customers' and prospects' critical business objectives. Because we have such a diverse experience base, our members are exposed to historical and trending issues and solutions that serve as growth insight for executive acumen, strategic literacy, social responsibility, servant leadership, and sales excellence. I'll share more about membership in Adaptive Sales University in the last chapter, or feel free to head over to WinningAdaptiveSales.com to learn more at any time.

Encourage. Raise the level of your game, and help others do the same. Every member will benefit from Winning Adaptive Sales's five guiding principles, one of which is "G-2-G" (Give-to-Get), where we use our voice to help you find yours in whatever growth initiative you are focused on. Our unique style of sales enablement, delivery, and collaborative facilitation engages you in a way that inspires you to execute and take action without fear or reservation. Your confidence and competence soar!

Winning Adaptive Sales uniquely leverages the select few historical sales practices that remain relevant in selling high-value solutions to customers who have complex decision cycles based on the constantly changing global business environment.

ASPs are empowered with significantly differentiated levels of business acumen, strategic literacy, leadership competencies, and insights that enable them to deliver value, consult with customers, and define solutions to address their customers' CBOs—avoiding becoming DSRs.

In the chapters ahead, I hope you will be connected, equipped, encouraged, and enabled to live a "Yes You Can" life.

CHAPTER 1

ADAPT—OR DIE

Sales is a life-or-death profession. Sounds a little dire, right? But think about it. You don't get paid for second place in sales. In fact, if you don't win a sale, you're losing money because of all the time and resources you've invested in pursuing that sale. So coming in second in sales is truly life or death (professionally).

That's why, as a complex-sales professional in today's world, it's crucial to discover and embrace a more relevant method of pursuing the art of sales. The teachings and techniques of Winning Adaptive Sales are a viable and valuable solution for success today.

At its core, Winning Adaptive Sales is about taking the lead in today's rapidly changing world of complex selling. Technology such as high-speed networks, mobile devices (smartphones and tablets), and social media services like Twitter, LinkedIn, Facebook, and others have obliterated the sales profession by enabling buyers to circumvent sellers. In a marketplace like this, it's critical for you as the sales professional to take the lead in the customer's buying journey, which puts you in the position to consistently win with Adaptive Sales.

FOLO—FIRST ON, LAST OFF

A key to Winning Adaptive Sales is for the sales professional to be a boots-on-the-ground leader. Whether you're a sales manager leading a team or a sales professional pounding the pavement, your role as an adaptive seller is to be the first into and the last out of any sales situation. This is a process I call FOLO, or first on, last off. Let me explain the power of this metaphor.

My inspiration comes from the leadership of retired Lt. Gen. Hal Moore, a recipient of the Distinguished Service Cross whose command as a United States Army lieutenant colonel in Vietnam was documented in his book (coauthored with Joseph L. Galloway), *We Were Soldiers Once . . . and Young.* His story was later made into a movie, *We Were Soldiers*, in which Moore was played by Mel Gibson.

As a boots-on-the-ground leader, Moore is perhaps best known for leading his troops through the first major battle between US and North Vietnamese troops, which took place in the la Drang Valley, a conflict that, in essence, set the stage for the rest of the war.

While the battle is certainly a point of recognition, what struck me about Moore's history was the challenging environment in which he led. At the time, the United States was already experiencing severe societal unrest from the civil rights movement. On top of that, what began as a peacekeeping mission in a country we knew little about escalated into a deadly war, inciting further societal unrest. In addition, those being drafted into the conflict didn't believe in what they were doing. Those soldiers had to be willing to put their lives on the line for something that, in their hearts, they didn't believe in—not an ideal recipe for engagement or commitment.

In the midst of all this was Moore, dealing not only with a growing racial divide but also with a draft that forced everyone together around a cause they weren't fully committed to or unified with. Just for a minute, put yourself in his boots: How would you organize everyone and get them to connect with each other and to a central cause?

In developing his troops and creating unity in this very emotional environment among the multiple races, ethnicities, backgrounds, and religious beliefs, a pivotal scene in the movie depicts Moore talking to his troops in a football stadium where they are surrounded by their families. Moore tells his troops that, "I can't promise you that I will bring you all home alive. But this I swear, before you and before Almighty God, that when we go into battle, I will be the first to set foot on the field, and I will be the last to step off, and I will leave no one behind. Dead or alive, we will all come home together. So help me, God."[1]

That's what FOLO stands for—first on and last off. A leader goes in first and then makes a commitment to be the last to leave. His or her example is paramount to commitment. In the battlefield we face every day in the world of sales, you must be the first on the customer's competitive business field and the last off that field if you are to win big. You must become the sales profession's equivalent of a Navy SEAL: the top 1 percent of all United States Navy personnel.[2] The symbol representing the Navy SEALs includes a trident—a similar trident is found in the Winning Adaptive Sales logo. That

---

1 | Hal Moore and Joseph L. Galloway, *We Were Soldiers*, directed by Randall Wallace, film (2002).

2 | "Learn About the Navy SEALS," Navy SEALS, 2016, http://navyseals.com/nsw/learn-about-the-us-navy-seals/.

symbol was chosen to encourage you to be a Trident Carrier—to execute every day in a way that places you in the top 1 percent of all sales professionals. I chose it as a way of inspiring you to always equip and prepare yourself for the sales battlefield, to commit to being the first on and last off, and to remember that unless you adapt in the chaotic world of sales in which we find ourselves today, you'll die as a sales professional.

DIVERSITY ON TODAY'S SALES BATTLEFIELD

Today, there's a different kind of diversity on the sales battlefield—a sales force composed of many different generations.

Predominant among these generations is the baby boomers, sales professionals who've spent their entire careers in the field. These seasoned sales professionals may have been beating the pavement for twenty-five or more years. They grew up selling and were taught business acumen and strategic literacy over time, because in their world, there was very little existing pent-up demand for the products and services they sold. As a result, many of them have been through class after class of training to help them perform to the best of their ability.

On the other end of the spectrum are young salespeople who are new to the industry. They don't have business acumen, strategic literacy, or experience in the field. They also lack really great communication and facilitation skills because they've grown up in a digital world; that is to say, they speak with their thumbs faster and better than they speak with their voice and body language.

In addition to the generational divide, the pace of change in business has never been greater. And if history is a guide to the future, the pace of change is only going to increase. Just like you, your customers are challenged every day by the pace of change. And they are starving for leadership to navigate those changes—whether or not they admit it to you or to themselves.

THE RISE OF ADAPTIVE SALES

The profession of sales dates back thousands of years. Before there was any semblance of currency involved, people bartered items, trading this for that.

One of the earliest documented sales methodologies—the idea of creating demand for a product—occurred in the mid-nineteenth century, when Chinese laborers building the First Transcontinental Railroad sold snake oil to the Europeans and other Americans, claiming that it would bring relief when applied to a site of pain on the body.

From the 1930s through the 1990s, there wasn't a lot of pent-up demand for products or services. Instead, salespeople had to generate that demand, and they were coached on newly developed sales methods designed to teach them how to do just that. That meant that salespeople had to get to know their audience, the environment, the sales territory or region, and even global events or trends that they were dealing with. Especially in the world of complex selling, these factors influence buyers. So having knowledge of the industry, company, competition, call point, and CBOs involved enables sellers to actually create demand for the products or services that they are selling.

But if you're a sales professional who grew up selling in the mid-1990s, then you witnessed the paradigm shift in big technology. You saw the rise of personal computing, client/server computing, and how end-user technologies, especially the proliferation of the Internet, began to enable consumers to make buying decisions via the World Wide Web. Sellers in the midst of all this change didn't have to create demand; they just had to react to existing demand with a somewhat competitive price over the competition and a better relational connection to the executive sponsors and decision makers—the salespeople with the best executive relationships and a competitive price in the 1990s won. Those decision makers didn't have knowledge of the impact on their company's performance goals and metrics if the purchased products or services failed to deliver as promised, so executive decision makers would purchase from the salespeople with whom they had the closest relationships with. That, they believed, would allow them to lean on their relationships with those salespeople to troubleshoot until a resolution was found. In today's buyer-empowered complex-sales environment, salespeople who predominantly rely on relationship-based sales skills are a part of a breed I've termed as a DSR.

During the boom days of the 1990s, demand-creation sellers— those professionals who had business acumen and strategic literacy— took their stratospheric earnings and either left the industry or were promoted to senior leadership positions with the hope of cloning their success to continue the hockey-stick growth experience in the 1990s. And because of all the high demand, corporations either slowed or stopped investing in professional development of demand-creation sales skills. Salespeople were just let loose on the market because they were selling so much in reaction to the existing demand. Promoting excellent sales professionals to leadership or managerial roles was not always the best strategy—particularly without the provision of leadership skill building and coaching.

Then in 2001, the dot-com bubble burst. Companies like Cisco saw its stock decline by 86 percent, and Amazon watched its

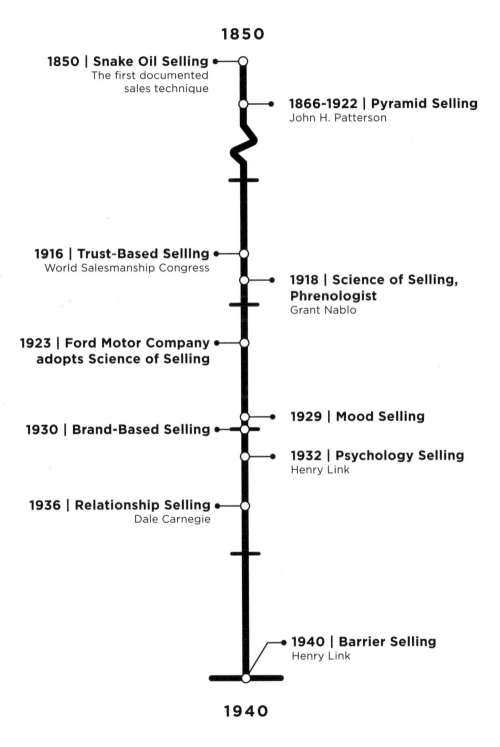

1850

1850 | Snake Oil Selling
The first documented
sales technique

1866-1922 | Pyramid Selling
John H. Patterson

1916 | Trust-Based Selling
World Salesmanship Congress

**1918 | Science of Selling,
Phrenologist**
Grant Nablo

**1923 | Ford Motor Company
adopts Science of Selling**

1929 | Mood Selling

1930 | Brand-Based Selling

1932 | Psychology Selling
Henry Link

1936 | Relationship Selling
Dale Carnegie

1940 | Barrier Selling
Henry Link

1940

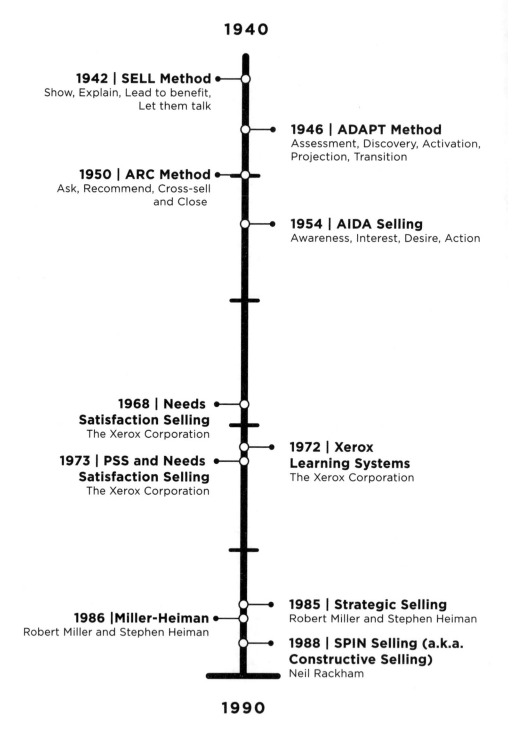

1940

1942 | SELL Method
Show, Explain, Lead to benefit,
Let them talk

1946 | ADAPT Method
Assessment, Discovery, Activation,
Projection, Transition

1950 | ARC Method
Ask, Recommend, Cross-sell
and Close

1954 | AIDA Selling
Awareness, Interest, Desire, Action

**1968 | Needs
Satisfaction Selling**
The Xerox Corporation

**1972 | Xerox
Learning Systems**
The Xerox Corporation

**1973 | PSS and Needs
Satisfaction Selling**
The Xerox Corporation

1985 | Strategic Selling
Robert Miller and Stephen Heiman

1986 |Miller-Heiman
Robert Miller and Stephen Heiman

**1988 | SPIN Selling (a.k.a.
Constructive Selling)**
Neil Rackham

1990

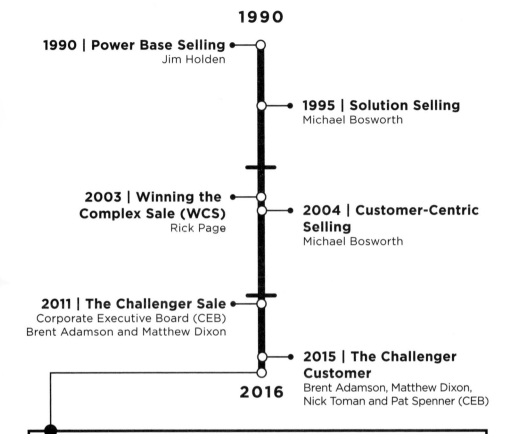

1990

1990 | Power Base Selling
Jim Holden

1995 | Solution Selling
Michael Bosworth

2003 | Winning the Complex Sale (WCS)
Rick Page

2004 | Customer-Centric Selling
Michael Bosworth

2011 | The Challenger Sale
Corporate Executive Board (CEB)
Brent Adamson and Matthew Dixon

2015 | The Challenger Customer
Brent Adamson, Matthew Dixon,
Nick Toman and Pat Spenner (CEB)

2016

2016 | WINNING ADAPTIVE SALES

Lee Hicks – Adaptive Sales University | Uniquely leverages the select few historical practices that remain relevant in selling high-value solutions to customers with complex decision cycles based on the constantly changing global business environment. Adaptive Sales Professionals (the new ASP) are empowered with significantly differentiated levels of business acumen, strategic literacy, and insights that enable them to deliver value, engage customers in a consultative way, and define solutions to address their customer's critical business objectives, stopping the cycle of the "Dying Sales Rep" age.

stock slide from $107 to $7 per share, and demand among buyers went away almost overnight. Those salespeople out in the field who didn't have business acumen, strategic literacy, or demand-creation selling skills started starving. With no demand, salespeople who lacked research skills and industry insights were just showing up and asking clients to educate them about their needs. They attempted to gain insights from the very clients that they were trying to sell to, just so they could meet their quota, earn an income, and (hopefully) retire.

It's no wonder that data sources like Forrester Research are reporting that business-to-business (B-2-B) sales jobs are going to disappear at an alarming rate. By 2020, according to one report, there will be in excess of 1 million fewer B-2-B sales reps employed in the United States than at present.[3]

Forrester breaks down these sellers into four archetypes: order takers, navigators, explainers, and consultants. Three of these archetypes will be hardest hit by the change in the marketplace: 33 percent of order takers, or some 550,000 people, will lose their jobs in the years to come; 15 percent of navigators, or some 150,000 people, will be out of work thanks to tools and integrations that streamline procurement; and 25 percent of explainers, or 400,000 sales reps who just convey information, will no longer be needed.[4]

So, old sales techniques that worked from the 1930s to the 1990s, such as selling features, functions, benefits, and even solutions, are going away. Tactics like "call blitzes"—dialing up anyone and everyone in a sales territory—are dead. Such tactics are known as *cold calls* for a reason—the salesperson commonly knows nothing about the person they're calling or the industry that buyer is in. Fewer than

---

3 | Hoar et al., "Death Of A (B2B) Salesman," Forrester Research, April 13, 2015.

4 | Ibid.

3 percent of cold calls actually reach a decision maker,[5] and only about 1 percent result in a meaningful contact.[6]

Yet even with those kinds of numbers facing them, the sales managers of today still can't see that twentieth-century techniques won't work with twenty-first-century buyers. They still believe the solution to a 1 percent cold-call conversion rate is upping activity—they want to increase the number of calls instead of warming up a call and making a "smart call" by researching and developing strategic insights. There is still a lack of training resources to help salespeople think critically and form hypotheses around business problems or opportunities. Without bringing those insights to the call, salespeople are burning out. And more critically, buyers are burning out as well—they're so frustrated with the process that they don't even want to take sales calls. As one who has been a sales leader, building on the experience of countless sales professionals before me, I believe that we must develop the leadership skill set and literacy of today's sales force. This is, in part, our opportunity today—to invest in sales professionals by providing leadership development, coaching, and consulting.

Now, while Forrester says order takers, navigators, and explainers are sales roles that are losing ground, sales consultant jobs are expected to grow by 10 percent, adding some fifty thousand jobs in the **All fifty thousand of those jobs will be filled by ASPs.**

---

5 | "Turn Cold Calls into Warm Calls," LinkedIn Sales Solutions, https://business. linkedin.com/sales-solutions/cx/16/01/cold-calling-demo-sem?src=go-pa&trk=sem_ lss_gaw_US_Search_Cold%20Call&keyword=cold%20calling&matchtype=p&veh=s3Ax 0p3PI_pcrid_106724057164_pkw_cold%20calling_pmt_p_pdv_c_&gclid=CLuGj4yu3c 0CFZA2aQodYUcI_g#!.

6 | Dale Lampertz, "Has Cold Calling Gone Cold?" Keller Center Research Report, September 2012, http://www.baylor.edu/content/services/document.php/183060.pdf.

same time frame.[7] I'm going so far as to suggest that all fifty thousand of those jobs will be filled by ASPs.

That's why twentieth-century techniques are being replaced by Winning Adaptive Sales techniques—this is what it means to adapt before becoming a DSR.

Winning Adaptive Sales brings awareness and insights to a business issue in order to get sponsorship of the executives who influence decision making and then lead the charge through the customer's buying journey. This message bears repeating: the key to Winning Adaptive Sales is ensuring the sponsorship of *executives who influence decision making*. In part, Winning Adaptive Sales picks up speed from the "Law of Big Mo," as explained by John Maxwell in his book, *The 21 Irrefutable Laws of Leadership*. The person who brings a CBO or problem to the decision maker's awareness is going to have the momentum to navigate the peaks and valleys of the customer's buying journey.

If you're still lining up to ask customers to map out their business problem so you can present a solution, then you're in danger of becoming a DSR, one of those million-plus salespeople who will be replaced by the year 2020.

TECHNOLOGY IS UPSTAGING YOU AS A SALES REP

Buyers already know what they want to know before you even get in the door. Why? Because nearly 75 percent of B-2-B buyers now say that buying from a website is more convenient than buying from a sales representative, and 93 percent say they prefer buying online to buying from a salesperson once they've decided what to buy. [8]

---

7 | Hoar et al., "Death Of A (B2B) Salesman," Forrester Research, April 13, 2015, https://www.forrester.com/report/Death+Of+A+B2B+Salesman/-/E-RES122288.

8 | Ibid.

Technology is everywhere, and it's enabling buyers unprecedented, anytime, anywhere access to the information they need to make their buying decisions. Just ten years ago, networks were crazy slow and smart devices weren't on a network. The iPhone, MacBook Pro, iPad, and Android didn't exist. And high-speed network access was a 1.45 megabyte T1 line for business, or DSL for residential!

Since then, more than two billion smart devices have hit ultra-high-speed networks, enabling buyers to gain ready network access to data, information, and insight into business problems. These devices are "smart" because of the applications that give users access to information in their buying journeys. Although LinkedIn, Twitter, Facebook, Google+, Pinterest, Instagram, and others barely existed ten years ago, today they're enabling three billion app users to literally look up anything, in real time, in the palm of their hand. Peers and analysts put insights online that buyers have immediate and easy access to.

So buyers are using technology to circumvent salespeople—to get away from dealing with nonvalue-based, self-centered, ignorant-in-my-industry salespeople. They're using the technology to identify what's going on in their industries globally. And they're using social media to inform themselves of the struggles of peers in their industry so they can become better in their own businesses.

In short, more so than any other time in human history, buyers are getting better information and support for their buying decisions from sources other than the sales professional. *That's a problem.*

As a sales professional, until you start using Winning Adaptive Sales's techniques to bring critical thinking to the data that your buyer is looking at, you're always going to be behind. That means you're not leading—the customer is leading. Even if you think you've won a deal, without insights into the customer's goals, objectives, and challenges—like those insights of Forrester's sales consultants, only the customer knows the real value of your product, because only he or she knows how big of a problem you're solving for them.

The situation isn't helped by the fact that, according to Forrester's 2015 Executive Insight Survey, there's a gap in the effectiveness of salespeople when they engage with customers. While Forrester's study found that 88 percent of executives surveyed said salespeople they met with knew the products they were representing, imagine the negative impact on the sales profession by the other 12 percent who don't even know their own products. ASPs go into every customer/prospect conversation prepared to break through a hardened heart or perception of salespeople.

The Forrester survey also found that only 55 percent of sales professionals knew what was going on in the executive's industry—nearly half of salespeople don't know what's going on in the industry of the company they're calling on. Sales professionals say they want to be "trusted advisors" to their customers. But how can they, if nearly half have no knowledge of a customer's industry, much less insights, experience, and ideas for growth that account for the trends and challenges in that particular industry? As professionals, salespeople require high-level and sustainable leadership skill development, a highly leveraged form of training that is not simply for the manager or the executive; it is for the sales professional who wants to succeed and remain relevant today.

Only 55 percent of sales professionals knew what was going on in the executive's industry.

Today, sellers must use technology to become as much of an expert as they can in every industry they're calling on. It sounds like a big task. While you may not be an expert, you can at least be literate.

FORRESTER EXECUTIVE INSIGHT SURVEY

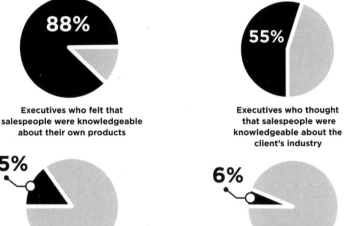

88% Executives who felt that salespeople were knowledgeable about their own products	**55%** Executives who thought that salespeople were knowledgeable about the client's industry
15% Executives who find their meetings with salespeople valuable	**6%** Executives who felt that the salesperson's agenda was to help them deliver results

Source: Source: 2015 Forrester Executive Insights Survey

SALES EXPERTS OR SALES LITERATE? A HEALTHCARE EXAMPLE

The complex healthcare industry demonstrates how an ASP adapts or dies based on his or her level of literacy. For example, when you're calling on the healthcare industry, you'd better know a few facts to demonstrate that you really understand the struggle that private practice physicians are going through based on the new burdens placed on them by the Patient Protection and Affordable Care Act (PPACA)—you know, the one Congress said was too big to read before voting to turn it into a law!

For instance:

> ➤ The Centers for Medicare and Medicaid Services (CMS) is using the electronic medical record (EMR) data on procedures to determine the volume of procedures. Based

on those numbers, CMS is determining how much is reimbursable for the procedure to the physician. So it's basically limiting how much money physicians can make from Medicare and Medicaid.

➢ Private payers like Aetna, Blue Cross Blue Shield, and Humana are no longer reimbursing at higher rates than CMS; reimbursement rates are equal to those set by CMS.

➢ Expenses of private-care providers have gone up dramatically because they're forced to adopt EMRs. Federal incentives for the systems are in the five figures, but the systems typically cost over $250,000.

➢ With forty-five million more patients in the healthcare marketplace now, speed is of the essence, but physicians were able to code procedures faster using written documents than their new EMRs.

➢ Improper coding can delay or eliminate reimbursements, so many physicians have turned to third-party providers for billing and coding services, further adding to their costs.

In short, physicians today are facing pressures they never foresaw when entering medical school and embarking on their dream career. Today, their revenue is capped, and their expenses are uncapped (and being forced upward), so their profitability is going down. To top it all off, in all but a handful of states, full tort reform has not been enacted, making physicians corporately and personally liable for any mistakes that happen—so their entire asset base, professionally and personally, is on the line as well. That's the profile of a healthcare buyer.

Similar profiles are what every ASP needs to know about every customer. As an ASP, you need to know the top three industry trends challenging the customer, you need to know or at least have a hypothesis about the top three CBOs of the customer, and you need to adapt your talk track to overcome the customer's challenges and achieve their objectives in a meaningful and measurable way. It is critical that you apply, at the very minimum, these three Adaptive Sales techniques to every complex-sales opportunity you pursue.

Figuring out what hits home with a customer means you'll have to rely, at least in part, on the Internet for up-to-date research, but that's what's required of ASPs who want to be sales leaders. Because if you're one of the 45 percent who doesn't have an in-depth understanding of the struggles your customers are facing,[9] then you're not bringing any immediate value to their day. You're just wasting their time.

Think about it: When you phone a potential buyer and tell them you're going to be in their area next week and you'd like to meet with them to learn a little more about their business, do you know how the customer interprets that? He or she is thinking, *Great. You want to take an hour of my time so I can teach you something about my company, so you can pitch me on your product, when you have no idea whether it's going to help my business be more effective.* By the way, that buyer is likely fielding calls from ten to one hundred other companies in other industries wanting to do the same thing; the phones of chief financial officers and other executive decision makers are ringing off the hook.

Cold calling is an epidemic; is it any wonder that the buyers are fatigued with the current performance of salespeople? We're conditioning buyers to hate our guts! That's essentially what the majority (94 percent) of respondents in the Forrester executive survey said—

---

9 | Hoar et al., "Death Of A (B2B) Salesman," Forrester Research, April 13, 2015, https://www.forrester.com/report/Death+Of+A+B2B+Salesman/-/E-RES122288.one.

that it felt like the salespeople they met with were only there to serve their own results and not to help the executive address the results of his or her business.

There are some historically proven principles that still apply to business effectiveness, especially Stephen Covey's *7 Habits of Highly Effective People* and *The 8th Habit: From Effectiveness to Greatness*.

Here are his seven habits, which are highly applicable to Adaptive Sales:

1. **Be proactive.** Be the first on the customer's business battlefield.

2. **Begin with the end in mind.** Have a documented plan to keep you on course.

3. **Prioritize.** Know what's important, what's urgent, and what comes first.

4. **Think win-win.** The first win is the other party's. If you can help the other party achieve a strategic win, your win is almost assured.

5. **Seek first to understand, then to be understood.** The most effective salespeople today don't talk about themselves, their companies, or their products first. They don't ask ten questions—that feels like a business interrogation. ASPs seek to understand the customer's position by applying insights and knowledge they derived from their research, analysis, and solution visioning.

6. **Synergize.** Bring your company's offerings to the table to address the customer's CBOs.

7. **Sharpen the saw.** After every customer engagement or communication, you must step back and assess the effectiveness of your leadership effort and apply improvements or corrective measures to ensure that you

remain connected to the right people with the right solutions to their CBOs.[10]

Covey's eighth habit is especially applicable: **Find your voice**. The greatest salespeople have found their voice by helping others find their voices. When Covey's habits are executed with confidence, they are a key to Winning Adaptive Sales and to success for all.

Another relevant metaphor Covey postulated in *The 8th Habit* is that, as salespeople and leaders, we're in a "permanent whitewater" business world where global competition, downsizing and rightsizing through lean techniques, process reengineering, new technologies, and more are making the environment so turbulent it's like trying to navigate Class VI whitewater rapids—the most challenging on the scale.[11] Covey wrote about this concept in 2004—imagine how much more "whitewater" we're dealing with today, with the introduction of billions of smart devices operating on ultra-high-speed wireless networks.

Unless you have a unique, content-rich, coach-led, and principle-centered process for adapting your selling style to the current demands of the buyers and how they're empowered and informed, you're going to be a DSR. This is why I'm suggesting a new paradigm—a new technique—to support our sales profession as adaptive. And IBAR is foundational to this technique, for both leaders and sales professionals.

INPUTS, BELIEFS, ACTIONS, RESULTS: IBAR

As a sales coach and event speaker, one of my most popular speeches of the past ten years starts with a simple question: When you woke

---

10 | Stephen Covey, *7 Habits of Highly Effective People* (New York: Free Press, 2004).

11 | Stephen Covey, *The 8th Habit* (New York: Free Press, 2004).

up this morning, did you say to yourself, *Hey, I think I want to be a little less effective today than I was yesterday?* Of course you didn't—no one wakes up in the morning wanting to be less of a performer than the day before. It's human nature to want to be better today than you were yesterday.

In order to become that highly effective ASP, you must think about the kind of results that you want in your life. You must challenge your thinking with a method that I've developed called IBAR, which stands for *inputs, beliefs, actions, results*. Let me explain this method in reverse:

> ➤ **Results.** If you want to have better results in your life—to go from effective to great with your customers—then those results are going to be driven by your actions.

> ➤ **Actions.** Your actions are all the things that you do—not the things your company or competition does. Your actions drive your results.

> ➤ **Beliefs.** Beliefs drive your actions. When you believe in something, you're going to take action. And when you take that action, then you're going to see the kind of results that come from a strong, committed belief.

> ➤ **Inputs.** This is what forms your beliefs. What you read, what you watch, who you listen to—all of the things that come into your head that you think through. Those inputs drive you to believe in something that you then act on, which then begins to produce results.

Inputs drive beliefs, beliefs drive actions, actions drive results. In order to achieve great results, focus on the inputs, and be surrounded, mentored, and inspired by great people! I saw IBAR in action in the hospital when my daughter was born weighing one pound, six ounces. At the same time, there were over one hundred other families in the neonatal intensive care unit (NICU) going through trials similar to those my wife and I were going through in dealing with our "preemie." In that life-challenging, health-devastating situation, the families that remained positive and took that positive energy with them into the NICU came out with the best results. By putting their positive energy and beliefs into the caretakers in the NICU, those families helped drive the actions of the NICU staff and everybody around them to better love and care for their children.

If IBAR works in one of life's most difficult crises, it can work in a business environment. It's made a big difference in this professional seller's life, and it's what's inside of Winning Adaptive Sales. Open your mind and your heart, and let the inputs of Winning Adaptive Sales come in and affect your beliefs to create an energy for you to act on. The results? A life-changing trajectory.

CHAPTER 2

INVEST IN YOU

Back in the 1970s and 1980s, before the boom/bust of the 1990s-2000s, major corporations like IBM, Xerox, AT&T, and ADP possessed an advanced sales-training mentality and made the conscious decision to create their own "professional universities." Their biggest investments were made into their most valuable assets—their people. They recruited people whose values fit the culture of the company, and then they put them through training to learn the company's way of doing things. This is where the phrase "I'm an IBMer" comes from.

The reason those organizations consciously documented their corporate DNA was to enable them to identify the personalities most likely to succeed in the company and who would also extend the culture and brand in the marketplace. To become an IBMer meant something—there was status tied to it. And to create really effective IBMers, the company invested heavily in the development of those people once they were hired.

I was blessed to start my career at Control Data Corporation (CDC), the former IBM Service Bureau Corporation, in the late

1980s after coming out of the University of Georgia with a bachelor's of business administration in finance. CDC resulted from a 1968 antitrust lawsuit against IBM that was settled in 1973. Although CDC was fully independent following the lawsuit settlement, the company maintained the IBM training traditions to assure its team was the best in the industry.

I was hired as a telemarketing representative, and my responsibility was to use the phone as a "power tool" to set appointments for the outside field reps known as "hunters." I always thought "shooters" was a better term for them because I was the one doing all the hunting—it was my job to target the right companies and the right person with power, to deliver a value proposition that generated a new sales opportunity.

The company spent a lot of resources teaching people business skills, everything from integrity and time management to critical thinking and knowing how to treat other people. In fact, my first class was in business ethics, and I was in training for six months before I ever made a phone call to a potential customer because the company wanted to ensure that every employee understood and lived the values and integrity that were foundational to its culture and reputation.

My second class was in business analysis to help me develop the skills to analyze industry trends, market trends, annual reports, quarterly reports, competitive trends, and so on. In other words, the company wanted to light a fire in each of us to always "have a heart for learning" so that our business acumen and strategic literacy would be second to none.

The company also taught us how to communicate. It taught us how to write a letter, speak on the phone, and connect with others through presentations in one-on-one settings, in groups, and as keynote speakers before hundreds or thousands of attendees. It also taught us how to build teams and deal with conflict.

The company also had a six-month sales training program that taught salespeople everything about the company's customers, its markets, and the industry. In other words, CDC built sales professionals because those people had to be taught how to generate demand in selling.

When we hit the information age in the early 1990s and corporations stopped investing in professional development, they turned instead to paying sign-on bonuses for the best demand-generation salespeople to come work for them so they could reap the harvest for as long as possible.

Unfortunately, because there was so much demand for products and services from roughly 1991 through about 2001, salespeople also stopped investing in themselves. So when the bubble burst around 2001–2002 and demand-reaction sellers needed to return to demand-creation selling, the skills were gone—and the development programs and platforms were gone as well.

Rebuilding those programs and platforms has been a slow process; while some companies have managed to close the gap and are back to building great business minds through their own programs, generally speaking, corporations still don't invest in the development of their people the way that they did prior to the 1990s.

If you're selling in today's environment and your company isn't providing best-in-class training and skill development, the only way to be the best in your game is to take ownership of your own professional development. And the first check you need to write is to yourself. That's the only way to ensure that you are positioned not just to survive today's chaotic world of complex sales but to thrive in it—to be in the top 1 percent of it, the Trident Carriers!

What does that self-investment look like? If you're new to the game, it means building up a strong foundation. If you've been selling for twenty-plus years, you need to rebuild based on the current conditions, in which buyers are more empowered than sellers.

At minimum, your goal must be to level the playing field. Ideally, you need to take control back—and that means investing in your Adaptive Sales skills and acumen. If you're not willing to write that first check for your own strategic-literacy and business-acumen development, then the question is: Why should anyone else write a check to invest in you?

HOW DO YOU GET BUSINESS ACUMEN AND STRATEGIC LITERACY?

How do you prepare to provide business insight, not just product insight, for the people you're trying to sell to?

Your first investment should be in data sources that will inform you about what's going on inside the industry and companies you're calling on. That resource needs to allow you access to daily updates on the industries that your prospects and customers live inside of.

Here are a couple of examples of what it means to bring insight to the customer-buying journey.

One of my current clients is a network hardware manufacturer—the company is the connector of all things voice, video, and data to the globe. Around the world, major telecommunications companies have networks built on this company's technologies. The company essentially sells to one industry, and becoming a specialist in one industry is typically not that difficult. But this company operates worldwide, meaning that it faces a whole host of political, geographical, socioeconomic, and other challenges in various countries. For its salespeople to have strong, insight-led conversations about solutions the company can bring to consumers, they must have the business acumen to know what's happening not only in the industry but also how the industry is affected by all the other market, geopolitical, and environmental conditions in which the company operates.

Ten years ago, the company had revenues of $300 million. Since deploying Adaptive Sales programs designed to keep the skills of the company's salespeople at the highest level, the company has become a $7 billion organization through organic sales and acquisition.

That's the power of Adaptive Sales. It's imperative for you to have business acumen and literacy if you're going to adapt and be seen as an effective and T-R-U-S-T-ed insight provider.

Another client of mine is a company that sells consumer-oriented and small- and medium-size business solutions. Its business-2-business (B-2-B) sales team works solely in the United States, but that team calls on small- and medium-size companies as diverse as law firms and nonprofits, retailers and restaurants, construction and transportation, manufacturing and financial services, and healthcare and veterinary practices, to name a few. It's common for the salespeople to touch five to ten different industries in a single day.

How can this company's salespeople be experts in dozens of industries? While it's practically impossible for a sales professional to be an expert in that many essentially unrelated industries, it is possible to be industry literate in all of them. Even if your turf includes everything from healthcare providers to trucking firms—markets with two distinctly different challenges—you can still understand what's pressing down on the companies operating in the industries you sell to and then see what challenges they have in common. For instance, you already know that cyberthreats are just as real to your small- to medium-size retail clients as they are to big-box retailers.

The sad truth, as documented by research conducted by First Data Corporation, is that 90 percent of all cyberattacks today affect small- to medium-size businesses; 71 percent are happening on companies with fewer than a hundred employees.[12] And 80 percent of small- to medium-size businesses that experiences a cyberattack—the theft of credit-card or personal data—close and are out of business because of that attack within eighteen months.[13]

Bringing real insights to your retail clients means information such as the effects that the new Payment Card Industry Data Security Standards (PCI-DSS) will have on their business. Most small- to medium-size retailers don't know even know about this contractual obligation, which they agreed to when they signed with the bank that is their merchant payment provider. They don't realize that their contract says they will comply with the rules and regulations of PCI-DSS, which states that they are financially responsible for losses incurred by customers as a result of a hacking. The merchant (your customer/buyer) is financially responsible for those issues—not the banks or credit-card companies.

This change occurred in October 2015, when merchants signed a new contract around the point-of-sale systems that accept EMV chip cards, and it means that now they are accepting the liability when something goes awry. This is an example of the kind of insights you, as an ASP, must research, understand, and bring to the table. As a sales professional, if you don't talk to a retailer about their risk exposure based on PCI-DSS and help them with solutions for their facility, people, and technology, you're missing out on one of the

---

12 | "Small Businesses: The Cost of a Data Breach Is Higher Than You Think," First Data Corporation, 2014, https://www.firstdata.com/downloads/thought-leadership/Small_Businesses_Cost_of_a_Data_Breach_Article.pdf.

13 | Ibid.

biggest drivers of buying decisions in today's small- to medium-size business marketplace.

Industry trends like PCI-DSS are textbook reasons to invest in your business acumen as an ASP. You need to not only have a deep understanding of your clients' pains but also be able to use that knowledge to help your customers operate and grow their businesses.

Without insight, acumen, and strategic literacy, you will be marginalized, and the customer will always have leverage over you. The customer will have control in the negotiations and will always use price to lead the conversation, and he or she will win. In other words, you will be the reason your prospects are stealing margin from your company, and that means stealing income from your W-2 because you didn't invest in your skills.

WHERE, OH WHERE, TO TURN?

So where can you learn about the trends affecting your clients' industries? What resources can educate you on the general, technological, and financial trends in the marketplace? Here are some of my top choices for achieving dramatic growth and expansion in your business acumen and strategic literacy:

> **InsideView.com.** For an annual fee, InsideView.com gives you the insight you need into your customers' industries. It can arm you with the data you need before you write your first e-mail to a business owner or a decision maker, before you make what would have been a cold call and will now be a "warm smart call" or before you have your first face-to-face meeting. InsideView can help you position yourself as a partner, not simply a vendor. The site helps you see the size, current challenges, trends, and structure of an

industry as it relates to suppliers, buyers, and new entrants. It can then provide you call-preparation questions, helping you start a high-level business dialogue with decision makers. If you're not using it and you're competing against someone who is, then they're going to have the "Law of Big Mo" against you—they're going to have the momentum.

> **First Research (firstresearch.com).** If you have deeper pockets and need deeper insights, First Research by Dun & Bradstreet can help you become an expert on a particular industry.

> **LinkedIn.** Are you tapped into the power grid of LinkedIn? If not, the next check you need to write is for a premium membership so you can unleash this social-selling and networking powerhouse. LinkedIn can replace traditional networking activities such as cold calling and events sponsored by Rotary clubs or chambers of commerce.

If you're using LinkedIn as a digital version of your resume, you're operating with archaic notions. People who are on LinkedIn looking for insights are not interested in your resume and job history. They're looking for what you've done with your experience to help others effect change, address objectives, achieve goals, and deliver results. Your LinkedIn profile needs to be not you bragging about you but you documenting the value that you've provided others.

The best way to do that is to have other people write recommendations for you explaining the impact you made in their business—in their world. Recommendations can raise your profile up and make it much easier to find you when people are out there searching for insights. There are few faster ways to go from e-mail to phone conversation to face-to-face meeting than by having LinkedIn help you gain trust with a call point by having someone say, "Take this person's call, I think you'll get value from it—I did!"

The Power Formula for LinkedIn Success, by Wayne Breitbarth, can coach you on how to use LinkedIn as a power tool. Think of it as an owner's manual to guide you in your quest for gold nuggets of opportunity on LinkedIn. The book can help you leverage the industry knowledge you gain from InsideView and help you connect to people in a way that will help you dramatically grow your pipeline.

If you aren't tapping into the power of LinkedIn and your competition is, you're going to experience the slow and painful death of your sales career. For instance, as documented on LinkedIn's website, LinkedIn Sales Navigator taps into the power of LinkedIn's 433 million-plus member network to help sales professionals find and build relationships with prospects and customers through social selling. On average, social-selling leaders experience the following benefits:

- 45 percent more opportunities created
- 51 percent more likely to achieve quota
- 80 percent more productivity
- three times more likely to go to their company's Presidents Club trip[14]

---

14 | LinkedIn Sales Solutions, https://business.linkedin.com/sales-solutions/cx/16/01/request-demo-sem?src=go-pa&matchtype=e%5D&veh=siLfSjeZq_pcrid_108245001364_pkw_linkedin+sales+navigator_pmt_e_pdv_c_&gclid=CK6dxYew8cOCFYlrfgodxrQEsg&trk=sem_lss_gaw_US_Search_Brand_Sales+Navigator&keyword=linkedin+sales+navigator.

While I highly recommend reading books filled with insights, particularly Stephen Covey's *The Seven Habits of Highly Effective People* and *The 8th Habit: From Effectiveness to Greatness* and John Maxwell's *The 21 Irrefutable Laws of Leadership*, I get it if you just don't have the time.

➤ If that's your situation, then **getAbstract.com** is a third investment that can increase your strategic literacy and business acumen across the global business environment. The getAbstract website is essentially a modern-day Cliff's Notes for all business-book publications; its tagline, "Compressed Knowledge," is apt. The organization pays writers to read business books and create a two- to five-page abstract that rates and summarizes the book, provides key takeaways and teaching points, includes notable quotes, and contains the author's biography. The summaries are quick reads that allow you to absorb the knowledge of the business books at a level that's detailed enough to let you execute on the information.

With getAbstract, you can become literate and skillful in the techniques that are recommended in the insightful business books in the market. It's a nominal investment for you to have at your fingertips—a knowledge base for linking to relevant topics with your customers. It will also give you a stronger base for telling stories and linking what you're doing into well-known best practices. For instance, if you can connect what you're trying to do to one of Stephen Covey's principles, then you'll have a stickier message for your buyer than your competition does.

Having compressed knowledge at your disposal lets you connect to thought leadership (the first T in T-R-

U-S-T) across all forms of business publications. Joining getAbstract will give you access to those insights to help you start having more detailed, consultative-oriented and subject-matter-expert-connected conversations. In other words, it will give you a McKinsey-like voice and mind. As one of the foremost management-consulting firms in the world, McKinsey & Company's points of view drive many of corporate America's strategies. Joining getAbstract gives you access to summaries that help you understand what makes a McKinsey & Company partner think, speak, and execute.

➤ **WinningAdaptiveSales.com and Adaptive Sales University.** Adaptive Sales University is a social-learning platform designed to serve clients and individual sales professionals who sell high-value solutions to customers with complex decision cycles. We make sure you have the business acumen, the strategic literacy, and the insights to deliver value, engage customers in a consultative way, and define solutions to address your customers' CBOs. Imagine Facebook meets LinkedIn meets Khan Academy meets SlideShare—that's the power of Adaptive Sales University. Memberships, which are available for individuals and for corporate sales teams, include access to a state-of-the-art social-learning platform with more than eighty courses in sales and service, leadership and management, and personal development. Also included in membership is access to the Birkman Method assessment, a personality, social perception, and job-interest report that measures and provides insights into your strengths, motivators, stressors, and career profiles.

Membership also includes Conversation Coach, a video-based simulation e-learning system designed specifically to build sales communications skills. Conversation Coach incorporates the latest video-based simulation capabilities that dramatically improve your skills and confidence in communicating with your customers, and it does so in a significantly compressed time frame. Conversation Coach creates great conversation muscle memory through practice on the Adaptive Sales University platform instead of in an actual customer meeting, which will prepare you for limitless success.

Investing in you is about combining the aforementioned resources to help you bring industry insights about the things that matter most to the people you're calling on. I'm sure you have heard the phrase "knowledge is power." I completely disagree. It's how you execute based on knowledge that creates power. Power comes from the art of closing the gap that Jeffrey Pfeffer, professor of organizational behavior at the Stanford Graduate School of Business, writes about with Robert Sutton in their best-selling book, *The Knowing-Doing Gap: How Smart Companies Turn Knowledge into Action.* In Winning Adaptive Sales, the art of closing the gap between insights and results resonates from the ASP's skill in "story selling," not storytelling.

Winning Adaptive Sales, InsideView, First Research, LinkedIn, and getAbstract help you target strategic industries and accounts, prepare your communication to connect with executives' CBOs, and deliver in the top 1 percent of all complex salespeople to become a Trident Carrier.

THE ART OF "STORY SELLING"

Call-point targeting and communication preparation are critical to a successful conversation with a customer. Targeting and preparation are most powerful when you can execute them in your unique delivery style. That delivery happens through emotional bonding, attention-grabbing tactics, and authentic communication—in other words, "story selling," developing a unique, differentiated, memorable, and unforgettable style of delivering experience-based stories.

Emotional bonding. Knowledge is not power. Information is not power. As I mentioned earlier, it's how you use information and knowledge in delivery that's going to determine whether it's powerful or not. Did your message strike an emotion? Did it connect in a meaningful way? Decisions are not *made* on a logical and rational basis; they're *supported* on a logical and rational basis. Decisions are made in a part of the brain that has no ability for language, that can't articulate. Decisions are made based on emotions, a discovery author Simon Sinek documented in his best-selling book *Start with Why.*

Once you have the right target and are fully prepared, then you must capture those efforts with a delivery that is provoking, challenging, and emotionally bonding. I must confess that early in my sales career at CDC, where we competed against the industry giant ADP every day, I fancied myself as a great presenter—and by most accounts, I was. But there was one particular ADP salesperson who had my number. No matter what I did, when I went head-to-head with him, I lost every time.

My prideful reaction was to believe that he had a trick or high-level relationship up his sleeve that he played to beat me. (Notice how I purposefully chose the word *reaction* versus *response*. Why? Because a *reaction* is instinctual, whereas a *response* is thoughtful.) However, it's important to note that he was one of ADP's top salespeople year in and year out, qualifying for ADP's Presidents Club all twenty-six years of his career.

Fast forward several years. I was working hard at D&B Software, seeing the returns in my W-2 and achieving the 1992 Rookie of the Year Award, when I received an invitation to my ADP nemesis's retirement party. I was shocked. I didn't even know he knew my name, much less where I was currently working. There were several ex-ADP salespeople in my D&B regional office, so I asked them if they received an invitation and if they were planning on attending. Their reaction was over the top: "We wouldn't miss it for the world. You're going, right?"

"No way," I initially responded—again, through my pride. "Why would I want to celebrate the career of a man who beat me 100 percent of the time?"

"Because it will be a blast," my D&B friends and associates replied, incredulously. "Clearly he thought enough of you to include you in one of the most important days of his life. And did you stop to think that you might learn something beneficial to your career and quite possibly your life?"

So I boxed up my pride and attended the retirement party of the man I deemed guilty of professional aggravated assault.

The party was in full swing when I arrived, and although it was ultimately one of the most memorable events I have ever experienced, I initially kept to the perimeter of the gathering; I didn't know many people there, and that old "Lee pride" was still creeping up a bit.

Let me pause and share with you a bit of an embarrassing truth: At that point in time, I still didn't actually know what the sales assailant looked like. Then a kind, soft-spoken gentleman greeted me with a firm handshake, saying, "Lee, I am so glad you decided to come to my party."

There I was, shaking the hand of who I thought should be a convicted business felon!

My first response to his greeting was, "To be honest, I almost didn't come, and I'm not quite sure why you invited me."

He replied, "Because in all of my years of selling, you were the most competitive and challenging opponent I ever went up against."

I honestly responded, "I can't imagine that to be the truth, seeing as how I never beat you a single time! You batted a thousand against every pitch I threw."

"Lee," he said, "that's why you are here. My sales career is over. Yours is just beginning. If you are open to it, I want to share with you what I did that enabled me to drive every one of your pitches out of the park. Can I share that with you?"

"Absolutely," I said, without thinking. I couldn't believe it—his style was so insightful yet humble that I, too, was immediately sold!

"Well, before I tell you how I sold against you, let me first describe your selling style," he said. Then he proceeded to describe exactly how I worked. Before I went into an account, I prepared fully on the company's history, mission, values, facts, figures, and on my product capabilities—features, functions, benefits, and so on. My pitch followed a very logical process, presenting everything that made CDC's offerings *factually superior* to ADP's offerings. I wasn't sure how he knew, but when he asked me to confirm his assessment of my style, I did.

"You got it," I told him, so he continued.

"You built a solid, fact-based, technologically superior, logical pitch, thinking it would hit the mark and win the customer's decision," he said. "Your only mistake was, you didn't connect your superior, logical pitch to the one thing that drives all human decision making—and that's emotion." His words stopped me in my tracks.

"ADP had an inferior product to CDC, but I was able to win every time against you. That is because I used the art of storytelling to connect to the emotions that drive decision making," he said. I couldn't believe it; it was all so simple, and yet I had been missing the target completely!

Then he did something that forever changed the way I tell stories. He asked me to wait while he went to a corner of the room, and then he returned with four items: a rusty garden rake, a well-soiled straw hat, a watering pail, and a pack of tomato seeds. I wasn't sure how he was going to relate gardening to the complex computer services that ADP and CDC sold back then, which were actually the first and oldest "cloud-computing" platforms that companies licensed to run their financials, payroll, and human resources. But I admit, he had my full attention at that point.

He started the conversation by telling me to stay focused on the story and that I would see what he had discovered to be the difference maker in his sales career. He told me that, when he went into a prospect's business, he challenged himself to think and act like one of the executives within that organization. With that in mind, he told me how he would tell his prospects a story about gardening—now note that he presented his story with such ease that it was almost like a small play. He said that, after the brief introduction, he would place his gardening hat on his head, put the tomato-seed packet and the watering pail on the table for everyone to see, and then hold the rake in his hand and continue his story. Here's the story he used with prospects:

> The decision in front of you is strategic to the growth
> of your organization, and the expected yield from

the investment in the operational systems is similar in nature to the yield of a crop of vegetables necessary to feed a population. Vegetables feed and nourish growth in people; operational systems feed and nourish corporate goals, objectives, and growth initiatives. As an avid gardener, let me demonstrate what it takes to get the greatest yield from your land.

The first thing you have to do is survey the land you have available and design the best layout for the types of vegetables you plan to grow. In replacing current business systems, you have to do the very same task of assessing the best design to deliver the greatest yield to the business. ADP's team of business systems designers and architects are the most experienced in the field and will be on-site for you from day one. Once you have a design for the land, you have to use your rake or some other tool to break up the ground to prepare the soil in a way best to receive the type of vegetables you will plant. This applies to your business systems as well. You will have to be prepared to get a little dirty because you will have to break apart your current systems and processes in order to prepare for the new systems of growth to be installed.

Once the ground is tilled and arranged in the proper rows, it's time to plant the seeds for your tomatoes, cucumbers, beans, corn, and squash. In business, this is where we develop and install the functional specifications and work flows required to run and grow the business.

> In gardening, once the seeds are in the ground, you have to water and weed the garden every day to enable the best growth possible. The same is true in business. You have to maintain, repair, and upgrade constantly to assure growth and the highest yield possible. That is what ADP does better than anyone; we partner with our customers to achieve the highest business yield possible.

Even I was captivated by his story! It's no wonder he had beaten me at every turn.

Attention grabbing and value driven. When delivering a message, your goal must be to immediately get the person's attention. As part of your self-investment, challenge yourself to find ways to make an emotional connection at the start of every communication with your client.

For instance, e-mails to prospects must have attention-grabbing headlines. How do you go about creating headlines that make someone want to read on?

Start by sitting down with no distractions. Then, based on the insights you've gathered during targeting and preparation, ask yourself, "What would make me want to read this headline?" What kind of headline can you put together that will make your call points stop what they're doing and want to read what you have to say? (Tip: The headline can't be about you; it has to be something that connects to them emotionally.)

Now, there's something of an art to creating headlines. If you aren't confident in your headline-writing skill, go back and examine some of the greatest headlines of all time and try to decide how they connected emotionally. For instance, when ice hockey player Mike

Eruzione made the game-winning goal for the 1980 US Olympic team in the semifinals, the headlines in the newspapers the next day didn't read, "Eruzione Scores." Those attention-getting headlines read: "USA Wins" and "Yes I Believe in Miracles." Not everyone connects with Eruzione or even the sport of ice hockey. But that simple shout-out by sports commentary legend Al Michaels, "Do you believe in miracles?" emotionally bonded and connected to a much broader audience; in fact, it connected with a global audience.

Attention-grabbing headlines won't get you very far without a value-driven message: What impact is the communication going to have on your target? It has to be a big impact. It has to connect in a big, meaningful, strategic way for it to create the emotion that the service or product is a "must-have," not just a "nice-to-have."

The goal of a written sales communication such as an e-mail is to set up the phone call that gets answered beginning a business conversation, grabs the prospect's attention, and connects to what is most important to them. Investing in your ability to deliver must also include developing a great phone voice. Have you ever listened to the voicemails that you've left? If you arrived home from work and had one of your voicemails in your inbox, would it stimulate you to return a call right now? That's the kind of voicemail you must leave. If you don't, your call points will be inoculated against you—they'll never want to take a call from you again. If you can't leave a message that evokes a must-return-call-now urgency, then don't leave any message at all.

Authentic and sincere. Because your ultimate goal is to communicate face-to-face, your in-person communication must quickly connect to your call points. To do that, you must communicate in an authentic and sincere way that resonates with what's important to your prospect and develops a rapid path for them to have a trusting relationship with you.

When bringing thought leadership to the table, don't just regurgitate what somebody else said—don't start with "I read your website." Instead, if you've read the company's website and it reveals that you're dealing with a competitively driven company, then your insights must begin with a provocative statement that says, "My company and I are the most competitive in our market space. That's what drives us. We're not competitive just to win but competitive to be out in the game, in the world, striving to be better, striving for growth. Even if we don't 'win,' we win because we grew."

A statement like this lets the prospect know you relate to them on their level. Don't tell them you know they're a competitive organization because you read it off their website. Instead, internalize what it means to be competitive, then apply that to your prospect's situation: "What competitive means for us is that we're devouring industry insights around the globe to look for trends that could be meaningful and impactful to our strategy and our ability to execute. Then we use those as inputs for our plans. I do that personally, but we also do that corporately." That's thought leadership (the first *T* in T-R-U-S-T).

Internalize what it means to be competitive, then apply that to your prospect's situation.

You must also build sincere relationships (the *R* in T-R-U-S-T) at all levels in a company, not just in your comfort zone. If you're a technology salesperson, don't just call on directors of IT because that's the language you speak fluently. You must also bring thought leadership around how IT is enabling the corporate goals of revenue or market share growth, shareholder value impact, or something even bigger. Even if you're an executive strategist, you must be able to synergize strategic solutions and conversations (the S in T-R-U-S-T) at all levels. You must be able to bring that conversation down to the bits and bytes and speeds and feeds of technology or marketing or service or sales or support understanding (the U in T-R-U-S-T) that's going to enable that strategy.

EARNING RESPECT

Becoming a member of the customer's team (the final T in T-R-U-S-T)—their trusted advisor—also comes from earning that individual's and that company's respect.

My dad was an elementary school principal for thirty years in Atlanta, Georgia, and he was loved and respected by students and staff. He knew the students by first name, and they would come up and hug him wherever they saw him. His teachers and staff also revered him; they didn't fear him.

He was a great CEO of that school because, for example, when Margaret (who ran the lunchroom) was sick and unable to be on the serving line, my dad, that revered leader, would put on a hair bonnet and an apron and take her place in the lunchroom serving line. Or when Miss Wells, the seventh-grade algebra teacher, was out with the flu, he'd go in and substitute teach. Or when Robert, the custodian, was unable to strip and wax the floors in the summertime or cut the grass outside, Dad would put on his work boots and his coveralls, and he'd get out there and do that work. In other words, as a leader, he could change hats and relate to every aspect of that school. He was a FOLO leader! (By the way, he did all this even as he worked on his doctoral dissertation and also ran a small business on the side.)

My dad's ability to relate at all levels, to bond with everyone instead of separating himself from the others he worked with, is what you must do as an ASP. You have to be able to relate to people at the top levels of the company all the way down to the people who write code, crank out spreadsheets, or turn wrenches.

The ability to relate to all levels of people comes from having a clear understanding of every aspect of the business, something I like to call "U-b-U," which stands for "Understand before being Understood." You can't go into meetings in a "tell" delivery mode, hoping your call points will educate you about them personally or about their business or industry. Today, you have to go into a call armed with that knowledge, because it's available on the web.

Instead, the understanding that you must search for is the impact that industry trends and challenges are having on the prospect's business. "You work here every day, leveraging all the resources possible, internal and external, to grow the business," you might say. "Based on my work with other executives running businesses in this industry, I understand what you're going through. But tell me how [current trend X or current challenge Y] is directly affecting you, your team, your organization, and your shareholders." Then you can transition into, "What current priorities and initiatives are you working on now? Are you open to some new suggestions about how to approach things a little differently to get a better return or see a better impact on your business?" Statements like these show clients that their business objectives come first.

Once you've had that meeting, then you must tailor the strategic solutions (the S in T-R-U-S-T) you bring to the table around the client's CBOs based on your relationships (the R in T-R-U-S-T) at all levels and your thought leadership (the first T in T-R-U-S-T).

That's how you become a part of your client's team. They won't even know that your business card has a different company name on it. You'll be a fully integrated, transparent provider to that team. Once you have that trusting relationship, you'll be the go-to person for your customer—you'll have an "in" that no one you're competing against has.

So what's next? Now you understand the importance of business acumen and strategic literacy, and you have some resources for gaining those insights. You also have some ideas for how to begin building a trusting relationship with clients. But there's one underlying key that can help you gain that trust quickly and efficiently. Wanna know what it is? Well, lean in. The next chapter begins the steps necessary to have that level of trusted advisor relationship.

CHAPTER 3

A HEART FOR
LEARNING THROUGH
"OTHERS FOCUS"

I n life, we like to think that it's our successes that define us. But success merely documents our perseverance; historically, success happens after many missteps some would call *failures*. Look at Edison's invention of the light bulb: He famously worked through hundreds of failed attempts before experiencing one success with the incandescent filament that allowed a bulb to burn consistently over the long term. In fact, Edison made over a thousand unsuccessful attempts to invent the light bulb. Yet when a reporter asked, "How did it feel to fail over a thousand times?" Edison replied, "I didn't fail over a thousand times. The light bulb was an invention with over a thousand steps."[15]

In truth, there are very few savants in our lives—very few people born with unbelievable natural skill—whether it's in music, math-

---

15 | Corinne Smith, PhD, and Lisa Strick, *Learning Disabilities A to Z,* (New York: Fireside, 1997) 262.

ematics, or science, or in communication and people skills, as is needed in sales. Instead, what makes most people great at something is their determination and passion along with their grit for getting through the struggles, challenges, and missteps. That's what enables us to be great. In fact, John Maxwell wrote a book titled *Failing Forward*, which talks about how analyzing our missteps accelerates us on our path to success. There's such a stigma attached to failure that we tend to want to pretend our missteps never occurred; but in truth, there are few teaching points to glean from our successes. Instead, if you go back and look at your missteps or mistakes, you can absolutely identify the tipping point where things went wrong; that's how to correct and ultimately succeed faster. By looking at your missteps and understanding their early warning signs, you can gain much more perspective and fuel for growth.

And by looking at your missteps, you may find that what's lacking is something I call "Others Focus"—the ability to sincerely place the needs and wants of others before your own. That starts with having a heart for learning; if you always have a heart for learning more from your missteps, those IBAR learning points will drive your growth. With "learning from our missteps" as a backdrop, let me tell you about a misstep of mine so epic that it forever changed my career and life trajectory. This is a story that demonstrates what being others focused, which you'll see is the key to success in Adaptive Sales, is not about.

In the mid-1990s, I was a senior account executive for one of the world's largest enterprise resource planning (ERP) software companies. The company had released a new client/server software product, and I was selling the HR application of that software because that was my area of expertise. Buyers were a bit uneasy about the HR application because the company I worked for was not based in the United States, and there was hesitation on the part of US-based companies to let a foreign company manage their HR operations, payroll, and tax calculations.

This was the era when sales were easier because of pent-up market demand, which led us to the rise of Adaptive Sales. The year was 1996, and I had already closed three major accounts, one each in the oil and gas, professional services, and airline industries. Because of those deals, I was well over my quota, so anything else I sold would pay me an accelerated commission rate, which at the time was around 20 percent.

I began working on a deal with the CIO of a major paper manufacturer. The company was already using my company's financial and manufacturing components, but its HR systems were from several other companies due to its growth by acquisition. As the calendar year was rapidly closing, I was excited to come in with a nearly million-dollar deal for that human-resources module of our ERP solution.

My sales strategy centered on the power of *integration* of products from the same vendor versus *interfacing* products from different vendors. In other words, *integration* delivered systematic and automatic data interchange, whereas *interfacing* required human intervention and maintenance, which was much slower and prone to errors. Since the paper manufacturer was using solutions from different vendors, its interfacing efforts were causing it a lot of angst. I was competing with two other payroll and human-resources leaders, both US-based companies. But, I argued, a payroll and human-resources system that integrated with our other components would allow full and seamless access to decision support for the expensive, human-capital side of the business.

As the year-end neared, the client asked me to bring in my manager, the executive vice president of sales, and we would meet over a five-star lunch in the client's executive dining room. "We'll have an eyeball-to-eyeball conversation, and we can talk this thing through before we make our final decision," he told me.

I was really excited that the deal might finally go through, so I reached out to my manager, who agreed to fly in for the meeting. He asked me to send him the account and opportunity-planning documents in advance so he could prepare for the meeting, but as this occurred before the Internet or e-mail really got going, that meant I would have to FedEx, fax, or snail mail them to him. So even though I told him I would send the documents, I was really busy at the time and just never got around to doing that.

My manager met me in the client's lobby thirty minutes before the lunch, and because I hadn't sent the documents, he asked me to bring him up to speed. As many of you know from experience, sales people affectionately refer to this as a "curbside review." I gave him the "Cliff's Notes" version: "It's a $900,000 deal, we're meeting with the CIO, and he has to do something because they've got to have an integrated solution. The deal is ours to lose," I told him.

"Okay, what else?" he asked.

"Well, that's about it," I said.

"Okay, then tell me about the CIO," he said.

"Well, he's a great guy," I said. "He's built a great team. He's excited about meeting you. He's lined up a five-star chef to give us a great experience. This is going to be awesome."

"All right. Is that it?" my manager asked me.

"That's it," I said. I was really pumped at that point.

We then walked to the elevators to ride up to the top floors of the company's fifty-story building as the lobby filled with hundreds of employees on their way out to lunch around town. As my manager and I entered the elevator, he said to me, "Lee, after you introduce me, I want those to be the last words you say."

What? That didn't make sense to me. I was one of the company's top performers—I was well over quota. But when we arrived at the dining room, I introduced the client to my manager, and then I went silent. The client looked at me to see if I was going to continue talking, but I held my tongue per my manager's instruction.

Even though I was really looking forward to that five-star meal, I remember very little about it. However, I do remember watching my manager execute one of the best strategic-business conversations I have ever witnessed. At the time, I thought I was good, but seeing him at work, I really started to understand how effective he really was.

Finally, we all stood up and shook hands, and the client said to my manager, "Thank you so much. It's now clear for me. We need to do this in a fully integrated way, and we need to do it with you. Lee," he said to me, "get me the paperwork. We'll get this thing done."

I was elated at that point! You know why? My mind was totally focused on that $180,000 commission I was going to get from the deal. I had recently married, and my wife had moved into my house on the golf course in the suburbs. While I loved living there, it was a bit of a commute for my wife, so she wanted to buy a $211,000 fixer-upper nearer to downtown. The commission from that sale would allow me to give my wife the home she longed for. So riding down the elevator, I couldn't wait to get out to the street and use a payphone to call my wife (cell phones existed but were still cost prohibitive). I couldn't wait to tell her that we were not only getting the house but that we'd be able to pay for it as well.

When the elevator reached the lobby, my manager and I exited and were once again going against the traffic—all those hundreds of lunch-goers were now returning to work. Then something completely unexpected happened. In the middle of that lobby filled with hundreds of people streaming in from the streets of downtown Atlanta, my manager stopped and asked me for my business card.

I handed it to him, and he looked at me and asked, "What's the most important thing on this card?" I didn't think my name was what he was after, since he had told me to remain silent in the meeting. Being a former University of Georgia cheerleader, I thought the company's name was the most important thing, and so I said—with spirit—our company's name.

"No," he replied. I was at a loss.

"What's your title?" he asked. It was senior account executive, which was my reply.

"That's right!" he yelled. It was like a bomb going off—all those people heading back to work stopped and began to circle us and witness the verbal beat down of a salesperson as my boss launched into a painful coaching session that changed the trajectory of my sales career.

"Account executive," he said. "I asked for you to send me your account plan, so I would know everything about this account. You didn't do that, so I had to get here early so you could tell me.

"But even then you didn't share anything that would bring me real insight as to what we might bring to the table to help them with their objectives. You didn't know anything about their revenue or profit trends, competitors, risk factors, growth plans. You knew nothing strategic about the account. And when I asked you about the CIO, you knew nothing about him.

"You didn't know his personal and professional agenda items, you didn't know the top three initiatives that the board was holding him accountable for, you definitely didn't know anything about his interests, hobbies, or philanthropic endeavors. He was a stranger to you."

My manager didn't stop there. "Since you didn't send me your account and opportunity plans, I printed off your expense reports to see if you were investing in your business acumen and strategic literacy like I encouraged you and the rest of the sales team to do at our midyear meeting," he said, pulling my reports out of his pocket. "Last year, I told you I would invest any amount of money in you to have subscriptions to *Forbes, Fortune, CIO, Wall Street Journal,* and other resources so you could start thinking like the executives that you're calling on and be seen as a peer and trusted advisor to them. But you're not expensing anything to give you more business acumen and strategic literacy. You are, however, happy to charge me for your Delta Crown Room, Marriott, Hyatt, and other club memberships so you can go down to the airport early and have your drinks, fly first class, and get top-floor service at hotels. You're happy to charge me for that, but you're not investing in yourself in order to become a more strategic business professional!"

"So here's the deal," he yelled. "I'm going to give you a chance to role play with me the meeting that I just led upstairs, and based on your performance, we'll determine whether you keep your job or not."

Wow! At that point, not only was I *not* thinking about buying my wife a house, but I was worried about keeping my job!

Thankfully, because I was so captivated with his delivery and execution in the meeting, I was able to pass the role play—which he did right there in the lobby. (Everyone clapped when he said, "Congratulations, you get to keep your job.")

But as we were walking out of the building, he told me that I wasn't getting the commission on the deal, so instead of calling my wife from a payphone, I got home as late as I could—she could tell something wasn't right. When I explained to her what had happened, she said, "The way he treated you wasn't right, but was he right with what he said?"

I said, "Yeah, he was right." To which she calmly and rationally said, "Okay, you can look at this and see yourself as the victim, or you can choose to realize that you just invested $180,000 in professional development that you'll use for the rest of your career." Wow, what a blessing to have such a strong and wise partner chosen for me.

That changed my life—I never went into another meeting, made another call, sent another communication (e-mail, letter, or otherwise) that wasn't others focused to the nth-degree. Anything I sent from that point on was as valuable and insightful as it could be about my client's industry trends, business goals, as well as his or her interests and desires.

That's what it means to be others focused. When you really focus on the bigger picture, when you focus sincerely and authentically on somebody other than yourself, a bigger energy than you comes back and rewards you many times over.

Being others focused also works outside the office. In our community, part of our little league baseball organization is what's called the Buddy Baseball Program, in which disabled players pair up with able-bodied players to compete and have fun. That program has really shed light on what's truly important not only for the players but also for some of the parents. In fact, one parent—who ultimately became the president of the organization—saw firsthand a tremendous change in his own son's life. His twelve-year-old, a baseball player in the little leagues majors, participated in the Buddy program. When the father experienced what that connection with a baseball player who had tremendous disabilities did for his son, it made him realize that the most important thing the Buddy Baseball Program does is create a sense of community where you are a small but important part of the greater, collective whole. It's not just about winning championships. It's not even about developing baseball players or a deep love of the sport. It's about bringing the community we love to those who have so much less than us. We love them more than we love ourselves.

That's the essence of being others focused.

"O" VERSUS "S" IN ADAPTIVE SALES

Historically, sales training has taught us to begin conversations with prospects by talking about who we are, what we do, and how we're different from our competition. But following that guidance, we would find ourselves somewhere on the continuum between being focused on self ("S") and focusing on others ("O").

If we are honest with ourselves, we tend to be much more "S" focused than we would like to admit. The natural bend is to be more "S" focused—survival of the fittest; look out for number one; me, myself, and I. These are the phrases that typically cross a person's mind, both personally and professionally, and perhaps especially in selling.

In sales, however, an "S" focus is very self-defeating. A typical, early "S" sales conversation with a prospect tends to be focused on data and statistics about the seller's company and the people running the business. It tends to be all about "you"—how big your company is, how bright or smart your people are, how many customers you have, how superior your products or services are, or how large your revenues and profits are.

If you were on a first date and your date heard you talking about yourself in a similar manner, he or she would probably be thinking, *Wow, this person sure loves himself (or herself)!*

Ultimately, all that self-talk amounts to arrogance in today's business environment. That's the last impression you want a new prospect to go away with.

In an early sales conversation, your prospect should instead leave with this kind of mind-set: *Wow! That salesperson was really prepared for our meeting. He or she really knows our industry, company background, current position, competition, challenges, and critical business issues.*

You also want prospects to see that you have experience helping other clients solve problems similar to theirs. In short, here's how "S" and "O" conversations break down. Do you see the difference?

"S" SELF FOCUS

- ➢ focuses on product/service capability
- ➢ a mastery of technical and competitive arguments
- ➢ seeks to win with features and functions
- ➢ emphasizes product presentations and demonstrations
- ➢ urgency to close

"O" OTHERS FOCUS

- ➢ focuses on business value
- ➢ a mastery of the customer's business problems or opportunities for growth
- ➢ significant industry knowledge that leads to credible recommendations

➤ maps recommended solutions to how they solve customer business problems

➤ urgency to deliver results to their bottom line

G-2-G (GIVE-TO-GET)

Being others focused is the guiding principle of G-2-G, one of Winning Adaptive Sales's five guiding principles. If you give openly, sincerely, authentically, with a loving heart, and not looking for anything in return, you end up getting back what you gave, ten times over.

G-2-G is the essence of T-R-U-S-T. If you want others to trust you, you must be willing to be fully transparent with them. That involves being willing to first share something with them that may expose your own vulnerability: for example, putting out a hypothesis, a point of view, or a perspective about your prospect. It's not about starting with a statement about yourself. If you go into a call talking about yourself—how great you are, the size of your company, your financial stability, your record numbers of quarter-after-quarter growth—the other party may understand your accomplishments up to that point in time. But what will really make you seem great to them is your ability to connect with them about their needs, to understand their motivators, and to demonstrate on some level that you are truly interested in their goals and objectives.

You can also show vulnerability by sharing stories of your missteps. For me, vulnerability is explaining how I invested the equivalent of $180,000 in my own personal development. You can view your missteps as either a curse or a blessing (with some of them, believe me, it'll take some time to find the blessing side). If you choose to see only the curse in your missteps, you're guaranteed to always be miserable and unhappy about that event. But if you choose to look for the blessing in your missteps, there's hope and a chance for growth. Personally, I would much rather have a chance at growth than a guarantee of misery.

The way to open up and give of yourself is to have a heart for learning—learning to be a better you, a more other-focused you, so that you can be better for someone else.

This goes back to investing in yourself but doing so with the understanding that ultimately you are investing for the others in your life. You must turn the investment in yourself into action. Bridge the gap between what you know and what your customer or prospect needs; knowledge will enable you to help your customer achieve his or her goals but only through your skill and ability to execute.

Without that investment, you're using hope as your strategy. And hope is not a strategy, as Rick Page, my former boss and partner, explained in his best-selling complex-sales book, *Hope Is Not a Strategy: The 6 Keys to Winning the Complex Sale*. Hope is a great strategy in life, regardless of your faith, but it's a terrible, futile strategy for complex sales.

How much should you invest in yourself so that you can sincerely and authentically bring real value to others around you? Studies show that, on average, companies in business-to-business product or services sales invest between 10.1 and 10.6 percent in marketing, which enables them to achieve a competitive advantage.[16] Equating that to your own skills development, how much better could you be if you invested 10 percent of your income into business acumen, strategic literacy, and knowledge? I suggest you consider investing

---

16 | Sarah Brady, "What Percent of Revenue do Publicly Traded Companies Spend on Marketing and Sales?", vital, https://vtldesign.com/inbound-marketing/content-marketing-strategy/percent-of-revenue-spent-on-marketing-sales/.

something between 2 and 10 percent of your income in helping you be prepared and enabled to bring real value to someone else.

If your income is $100,000, then you must be willing to put at least $10,000 of that back into yourself every single year to improve yourself.

If that seems daunting, compare it to other highly compensated professions. As I write this, the Masters tournament is taking place in nearby Augusta, Georgia. There's a reason the golfers arc called "masters," and it goes back to the investment they've made in themselves, which enables others to invest in them as well—sponsors, for instance, can invest in them and trust in a high return on that investment.

If your income is $100,000, then you must be willing to put at least $10,000 of that back into yourself every single year to improve yourself.

It's the same with any sport or athlete, whether it's a NASCAR driver, a National Football League player, or a Major League Baseball player. Top athletes invest a significant portion of their income into their conditioning, mental stability, nutrition, physical and psychological fitness, and skills coaching. Whether it's a swing coach in golf or a batting coach in professional baseball, athletes invest their money in themselves so that they can be prepared to make millions by serving others—their fans, sponsors, and teammates. Those who put team and others first—whose goal is to grow as a combined unit—are the ones whose stories aren't just told; their stories resonate and connect with the masses in such a more intimate, detailed, impactful, and legendary way.

When you see the value of investing in yourself work in other areas of life, then you must also see how it can work for you in the complex-sales arena. Because I can't disagree more with the adage, "It's not personal, it's business." I believe that everything in business is personal! A person works in a business for personal reasons. The business has no pulse. It's the people, collectively, that come together to create the pulse of the business; everything in business is influenced and informed by personal motives, agenda items, and desires and goals. At the end of the day, every business is that business because of the people who are in it.

And let's face it: We all want someone alongside us to help guide us. We want others we trust to coach us so that we can be our best. We desired that from our parents, and we still desire it as adults, whether from our church, friends, significant others, mentors, or bosses.

Being coached means that you must be willing to put your ego, self-centeredness, self-consciousness, or self-obsessions aside so that you can focus on something bigger than you. You can open up and really see the magnitude of impact that's available to you in your life.

DEATH TO SELF

If you're still struggling to understand what I mean by others focused, stop for a minute and think about how someone else put your needs ahead of their own and made a difference in your life. I remember very clearly someone who did this for me, and it not only gave me comfort at the time but helped me ultimately gain a global outlook on life.

As the offspring of an elementary school principal in Georgia in the late 1960s and early 1970s, the farthest I got from home was traveling by car to the Gulf Coast in neighboring Florida. It wasn't until college as a member of the University of Georgia cheerleading squad that I stepped onto my first airplane. I was terrified of flying, and when the pilot of that chartered plane sensed my fear as he was helping us load onto the plane, he said, "You're scared."

"I'm scared to death," I told him.

"Listen," he said. "I'm the pilot of this flight, and there's nobody on this plane that wants to get to our destination safely more than me. I can promise you that I'm going to put your desire for safety first and foremost.

"But what I want you to focus on is not the safety of the flight. Instead, I want you to focus on how big of a world there is out there for you to experience. Don't fear it, embrace it. For it can provide input that redefines what becomes of your life and how you live it."

Compared to six hours in a 1974 Ford Thunderbird traveling from Atlanta, Georgia, to Panama City Beach, Florida, the fifty-minute flight to Lexington, Kentucky, to cheer the University of Georgia Bulldogs on against the Kentucky Wildcats basketball team was a blink of an eye. The pilot was right! There was nothing to fear—and the world to gain!

That experience profoundly changed my life. That others-focused pilot wanted me to have the best experience. His words made me want to travel the world, which encouraged me to be in sales and to find inputs that would develop my thinking and that I'm now sharing with you.

However, when I was a young sales professional just starting out, I still had a somewhat sheltered outlook, which turned into a prideful view of myself. Working for big corporations, traveling all over the world, and seeing a phenomenal career bud and bring me more money my second year out of college than my school-principal father made left me believing that my career and the money defined me. That's how I presented myself to the world—in business and in personal relationships. I thought that by talking about my accomplishments on a date, I was demonstrating how I was a great catch—someone who could be relied upon to be a great provider. Instead, my actions became the basis for superficial relationships because it was all about me—I was a "Me Monster," a term coined by stand-up comedian Brian Regan.

Once I began to change and become more others focused, people who knew me well noticed the difference. One of those people was Rick Page, who I mentioned earlier. "Lee, you're starting to get it," he said to me one day at lunch. He told me that when I focused more on customers and how I could use my experiences and knowledge to bring them insight and impact, then I'd really start to see a more rapid path to strong, trusted business and personal relationships.

"Die to your self," he told me, which really means *live for others!* "Sincerely and authentically care more about the needs, interests, goals, and desires of the other person you're working

Live for others!

with in your personal and professional lives, and you'll start to see a return on that focus."

THE INTIMACY OF OTHERS FOCUS

When you really focus on the goals and objectives, drivers and trends, and challenges and obstacles of the person you're working with, then you can become an agent of positive change in his or her life. Focusing on others sets you firmly on the path to a relationship built on T-R-U-S-T.

If you were to visualize the level of T-R-U-S-T I'm talking about in a personal relationship, it would be that point where you're first holding hands with your significant other, where your fingers interlock and the chills run down your spine. That point where you are forever changed from the inside out.

That's really the kind of professional relationship that owners of small- to medium-size businesses, as well as executives of Fortune 1000 publicly traded companies, are looking for in partners and third-party vendors in their extended supply chain. They're looking for that business intimacy where they are willing to really open their professional hands up and interlace their fingers with another company.

Neil Rackham is a great sales and marketing thought leader who is behind the world-renowned sales methodology known as SPIN Selling. In his book with Lawrence Friedman and Richard Ruff, *Getting Partnering Right*, Rackham said that a strategic partnership is like a three-legged stool, and all three legs must be placed properly beneath the stool for it to uphold the partnership.

Those three legs, Rackham says, are common vision and values, intimacy and transparency, and a positive impact on both sides of the partnership. If the two sides of a partnership don't have a common value base or vision for the future, then they may work together, but they won't do it forever. As a seller, that begins by being others focused. If you're the seller in that partnership, then without understanding and sharing in the vision and values of your customer, you can look for that relationship to be a short-term one.

Intimacy, the second leg of the stool, is about both parties giving of themselves and being fully transparent. For the buyer, that means sharing current and future CBOs. For the seller, intimacy is about full disclosure of what they believe is happening in the industry and what solutions they can bring to address those needs and issues. Intimacy is also being willing to recommend the right solution, even if it's with another company (including competitors).

The final leg is that both sides have to see a positive impact in order for the partnership to work; for instance, margins can't be crushed down to where there are no or low benefits on one side or the other.

In order to have a meaningful partnership with your customer, you must be one of those Trident Carriers, that 1 percent of ASPs with whom clients can be transparent about their challenges and goals. That comes in part from being transparent with them about your capabilities of enabling them to achieve their goals and objectives. When you authentically G-2-G, you create that partnership—that bond—with clients, and then they'll become proactive in your relationship. They'll want you to come in as a source of ideas to help them operate and grow their business. You'll be a part of the annual strategy and planning sessions that the company undertakes to look at past successes, current market trends and issues, and future challenges and growth opportunities.

THE BUSINESS BACKBONE

Becoming an extended part of your customer's leadership team for the long term can apply to businesses of all sizes. In fact, never underestimate the power of Adaptive Sales with small- and medium-size businesses—these are the backbone of the US economy. Most small- and medium-size business owners are individually funding their companies—their livelihoods are at stake, as are the livelihoods of the people who depend on them for an income and a future.

Owners of small- and medium-size businesses are just as focused on success and planning as the largest companies around the world. In fact, planning for them is more important, because if something goes wrong, they're not just losing their job, they're losing everything—their savings, their real estate, their assets, and even their legacies.

The power of Winning Adaptive Sales can help strengthen that backbone of American business when ASPs bring insight-led growth opportunities based on their experience and preparation. In fact, according to 2012 US Census Bureau data and the Small Business & Entrepreneurship Council, the share of businesses with fewer than twenty employees is 97.9 percent![17]

Small- to medium-size business owners are starving for leadership from people who are others focused. They need outside professionals to bring real insight into their industry—not just knowledge but also a point of view, a way of thinking that challenges the way that they've been thinking and brings new, innovative ideas that can address what's really pressing down on them or stressing them out. They need outsiders to help them design growth plans that can be achieved.

What they don't need is someone to come in and ask, "What keeps you up at night?" That would be like going on a first date and saying, "Hey, how about we start by you telling me all the things that you struggle with in your life, whether that's an addiction to alcohol or huge gambling debts or some other dark disappointment?"

You would never do something like that personally, so why would you do something like that in business? That would be like calling out your client's failures—is that really a great way to begin a relationship? It's not human nature to do that, but salespeople are still being trained to have that level of first conversation.

Imagine the impact if you began a relationship by saying, "Here's the experience I've got in your industry. Here are some of the chal-

---

17 | "Small Business Facts & Data," Small Business & Entrepreneurship Council, accessed June 3, 2016, http://sbecouncil.org/about-us/facts-and-data/.

lenges that other leaders in your industry are working through, and here's how we've helped them do that." Then, they might be comfortable telling you about what's going on inside their organization.

Again, strong business acumen, strategic literacy, and being a trusted advisor are all trumped by your ability to be others focused. You must use your strategic insights to become a trustworthy resource for your client, delivering thought leadership in your client's industry and market by communicating across all levels of your client's organization, no matter its size. What's really driving your prospects? What unspoken needs or motivators are driving their strategy? What's driving what they do every day in their business? Answering these questions sincerely and authentically, without an ulterior motive involving self-gain, is how you build a long-term partnership with your client.

Now that you have some insight into *what* to do and *how* to do it, let's look at when to engage with your clients for the best outcomes.

CHAPTER 4

THE KEYS TO THE KINGDOM—WANT 'EM?

f you could know exactly where every one of your customers or prospects are in their buying journey, how valuable would that be to you? Having access to that information when you begin your engagement is, you'll discover, "the keys to the kingdom."

Even the most extensive coaching and most-perfected sales activity checklists and guideline processes don't guarantee the successful closing of a sale. Rarely do they really even influence it. That's because your sales activity is only as good as its alignment to the customer's buying journey.

Especially in complex sales, every customer goes through a buying journey that follows a consistent process. The customer may not even realize he or she is following this journey, but through my work at DSG Consulting and Kodiak Group, it's been captured and documented after assessing tens of thousands of complex buying processes.

That consistent buying journey is documented in what's known as the *S-curve* which can be defined as a type of curve that shows the growth of a variable in terms of another variable or variables.

CUSTOMER—BUYING JOURNEY

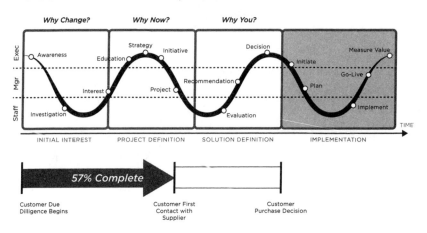

Source: DSG Consulting; Kodiak Group; Sales Executive Council, The Five Chapters of Executive Selling, The Era of Insight Selling, Nov. 16, 2012

The S-curve demonstrates how the customer's buying journey begins at a high point. Buying journeys in organizations large and small start when an executive or owner of a business becomes aware of a business problem or a business opportunity. If it's a business problem, the business leader is going to want a resolution. If it's a business opportunity, the business leader is going to want to pursue it for growth. The awareness phase typically comes to executives or owners not because they're the smartest person in the organization; it comes to them because of the inputs they're receiving—the insights they're getting from others around them. Those insights can come from a variety of sources: studying the industry, reading trade magazines, reaching out to CEOs of other companies inside or outside their industry, or listening to their management-consulting partner. That partner can be a big firm like McKinsey or Accenture or just an advisor who's been a mentor to them for years.

Ideally, you'd think that the awareness of a company's business problems or its opportunities for growth would come from the team that works within the organization—other managers, subject-matter experts, or staff. Unfortunately, that rarely happens. Too few organizations run their businesses the way that Jack Welch ran GE for years—by telling the management team and staff: "I want unfiltered candor from you at all times. I want to know what you see as either the opportunities for growth or the problems that are going on in our business. Don't just bring me challenges you're seeing, bring me challenges and opportunities along with your ideas for how to address those. Bring me your research and data and partnerships that can help us grow." It's all too rare that this actually occurs, because it's just not human nature for midlevel managers to feel confident going to an authority figure with what might be considered bad news or problems.

But research shows that 70 percent of all purchases by businesses today are made to solve a business problem.[18] So ASPs must consider not only what problems are facing customers but also who is bringing the insight around those problems to the executive or the owner of the business. This is because the person who is credited as the initial source of insight has a better path to executive sponsorship and T-R-U-S-T than any other competitor, and if a leader is not getting the right type of insight from internal staff to solve problems and take advantage of opportunities, then going outside the organization for answers will become necessary. The leader is going to look for others to assist on staying on top of what's really important in order to grow the businesses for which he or she responsible.

18 | The Successful Sales Manager, http://www.thesuccessfulsalesmanager. com/2014/06/70-of-people-purchase-to-solve-problem.html.

The awareness phase is where ASPs who have become very literate and developed strong business acumen around the industries they're calling on have a leg up on DSRs. ASPs who understand the CBOs relevant to the person and industry they're working with will be better equipped to connect, regardless of the operational focus of that person. Those ASPs will be able to bring awareness to new opportunities for growth or to resolve business problems, and they'll be able to get face time with owners and executives of any size of business. Owners and executives will free up their calendar wholeheartedly to an ASP of an organization that can bring real insight into problems they may be experiencing or opportunities that they should be taking advantage of.

Whoever brings awareness of that problem or opportunity to the executive or business owner will have momentum on his or her side, which as I mentioned earlier is what author John Maxwell calls the "Law of Big Mo." As you can see from the graphic, you're going to need momentum to navigate the valleys of the customer-buying journey. If your starting point is low in the customer's organization structure, it is an uphill climb, with you pushing your value proposition like a huge boulder, to the executives who create the company's strategies and fund those initiatives. One slip up and down you go, with the weight of the deal crushing you. But if you're the one bringing momentum to the customers as they navigate the buying journey, you'll be the one with leverage. You'll have the opportunity to create the strategy and the processes for addressing new opportunities and solving problems.

So what exactly are the keys to the kingdom? *Knowing that your customer follows a defined buying process or buying journey whether they know it or not and then understanding where they are in their buying journey.*

The S-curve can give you complete insight into the journey. You can use the S-curve graphic to understand exactly where every decision maker in the organization is in their buying journey, whether they're an executive, a manager, or a staff member. When you understand the customer-buying journey, then you can appropriately map your selling activities and adapt them to align your strategic solutions (the *S* in T-R-U-S-T) to that CBO or problem that your prospect is trying to solve. And you can align your sales activities to where your prospects are in the customer-buying journey.

So what exactly are the keys to the kingdom? Knowing that your customer follows a defined buying process or buying journey whether they know it or not and then understanding where they are in their buying journey.

Even if someone else in the organization or an outside competitor brings awareness to the decision maker, the S-curve can give you leverage by helping you identify the point at which you are entering the customer-buying journey. Then you can potentially bring new insights that could change the level of competitiveness and bring it around to your favor. You can bring in your strategic literacy and business acumen and not only address the issues that were already introduced by someone else but also be able to bring new insight to new issues that you uniquely connect to and that your competition is not aware of.

THE CUSTOMER-BUYING JOURNEY

Come along with me now as I take you through the customer-buying journey.

First, a couple explanations of the S-curve. The staff, management, and executives represent the call point or target audiences in your prospect's organization. The dotted horizontal lines reflect their levels in the organization; the S-curve demonstrates how the journey touches various target audiences throughout the buying process.

Columns in the graphic are labeled: "Why Change?", "Why Now?", and "Why You?" These are the three buying questions a customer asks in the journey; the questions evolve as the customer advances through the process from initial interest, to defining the project, to defining the solution.

Finally, the S-curve demonstrates the various critical points in the journey and clearly shows you whether those points are part of an uphill climb or a downhill trajectory.

Are you starting to get an idea of how important it is to have momentum on your side? All right, let's go.

Why Change? When an executive or an owner becomes **aware** of a business problem or opportunity, the real question the individual is asking in the buying journey is: "Why would I do something different tomorrow than I'm doing today?" The answer to that question is never just price, in spite of what salespeople in today's complex selling world commonly believe. *Price does not drive the decision.* Price may substantiate, support, or inform a decision, but it doesn't drive a decision. The price of a product or solution is not the early driver in an executive looking at making a change in what to do tomorrow compared to what they do today.

What drives a decision is traditionally a strategic initiative—something at a higher level that is driving that business owner or leader. That strategic initiative may be about creating or gaining a competitive advantage, addressing revenue growth needs, or addressing margin growth requirements. There might be an employee churn or loss number that's affecting the business, forcing the leaders to rethink how they're going to market and what they're doing. Or it could be something especially high level, like complying with regulatory requirements while still driving revenue growth to meet shareholder demand.

If the executive decision makers are asking, "Why change?" because they have become aware of a business problem, then they'll go down into the organization's management and staff to begin looking for answers. They'll ask their managers and staff to **investigate** potential suppliers or solutions to similar types of business problems or opportunities.

At the investigation phase, a request for information (RFI) might get issued or published. RFIs typically go out to maybe ten companies that have offerings they could bring to the table to address the business problem or opportunity. Based on that investigation, the staff, also known as *subject-matter experts*, will become **interested** in some of those solutions. And based on that interest, they'll go back to the executive team and **educate** them as to what their investigation found.

Why Now? Education in hand, the executive leadership team then holds a closed-door session to determine how the situation compares to the strategic plan that the organization is operating under. If the issue is not something that was in the budget, then the team must answer a question: Is the problem or opportunity **strategic** enough for us to do it right now? Even if the team decides the change is needed strategically, it still needs to decide whether there will be an impact on the business if the change isn't made right now. How does that impact compare to the established strategic plan? Is the change or solution a "must-have," or a "nice-to-have"?

The moment the change is determined to be a must-have, the executive leadership team assigns an **initiative** to an "owner." Someone in the leadership or ownership structure is assigned to "own" the initiative and to be held accountable for delivering the metrics and the impact on the business. That executive sponsor—the executive who owns the initiative—can create the strategy and bind the company. When the numbers are achieved, that executive gets all the praise and glory. If the numbers are not achieved, that executive is going to hold the bag for accountability because that initiative didn't deliver on its intended impact goal.

With the budget for the initiative approved and secured, the executive sponsor then assigns someone on the management team to oversee the details of the **project** to ensure that it is executed properly. The project manager defines an entire charter, with project requirements, that may include a detailed request for proposal (RFP) that is sent out to the initial lists of vendors that were investigated. The RFP is followed up by formal requests for an evaluation process to occur.

Why You? In the **evaluation** phase, the project is being managed, which leads to a detailed evaluation of potential partners and providers. That evaluation follows a very logical and rational process that includes demonstrations, site visits, reference checks, customer visits, and so on. A checklist, or scorecard of sorts, is developed to allow for a comparison of the various potential partners or providers in order to determine the winner.

Equipped with that information, the management team is able to make a **recommendation** for the organization to partner with or buy from the leading candidate to solve that problem or address that opportunity.

It's important to note, however, that in this phase, the buyers sometimes call up the salesperson to report that the deal is theirs except for one component. For instance, the buyer might call up the salesperson and say, "Your company brought the best product to the table, but your price isn't competitive. We need you to sharpen your pencil, and the deal is yours to lose." Now in that scenario, what the DSR heard was, "Congratulations, the deal is yours." That DSR is already dancing when he or she hangs up the phone; the DSR may even be calculating his or her commission at that point. But the truth is, right after the buyer hung up, he or she also called a couple of the other sellers involved in the evaluation and had the same "yours to lose" conversation with them.

The buyer does this because he or she needs a Best Alternative to a Negotiated Agreement (BATNA)—a backup plan, so to speak. That way, if the first or even second deal falls through, the buyer still has other candidates who can accomplish the goals and objectives on some level.

Knowing that the buyer has a BATNA, my advice is to develop a BATNA of your own. As the seller, you should have an early-stage negotiating checklist around areas that you can negotiate other than price. What can your organization offer that will allow it to hold its price so that it can get a fair margin, no matter what? How can both buyer and seller win in the negotiation? Having the keys to the kingdom—an understanding of the buyer's journey—can also help you gain insights into how big of a problem you're helping the customer solve. Without that, when the customer says the price is too high, you won't have any leverage for negotiating and all you'll be able to do is discount. You'll lose margin for your shareholders, and that's not a win-win.

Once the recommendation phase has solidified, the process goes back up to the executive team for a final **decision**. The commitment point comes when a decision is made. However, when customers sign on the bottom line of a contract, they are never jumping for joy—that's not their emotion. In fact, customers typically tense and tighten up when they sign the contract, because now they're at risk until they can actually build out the implementation—design it, go live, and then measure the value of their decision against their business problems or objectives.

Now let's get real here. It'd be great if those executive-level decisions were actually based on the logical and rational project plan and evaluation process, but in fact, that's never the case. As I mentioned earlier, according to Simon Sinek, decisions are not made in the part of the brain where logic, rationality, and language exist; there's no capacity for language to articulate why you're leaning the way you are. That's why people making a decision often say, "I don't know why, but it just feels right. It's a gut instinct."

Well, as we now know, it's not your gut that's making the decision. It's the part of your brain where decisions are made based on emotions, and what drives emotion is the connection to feelings of security—not facts, figures, and data.

THE EMOTIONAL CONNECTION WINS

As the ASP, your proposals and documentation must be logical and rational. But if you think that the logical best-price-and-feature-function list is going to win your deal in today's buyer-empowered world, you are in danger of becoming a DSR. In other words, the winning bidder will be the one who goes beyond a logical connection to connect emotionally and resonate with greater impact.

In the customer-buying journey, the ASP wins when he or she is others focused, when he or she connects in an emotional way that says to the buyer, "As a partner to you, we don't win when you sign a contract—that's not where we celebrate. We win when you can measure the value of your decision against the business objective that you bought our solution to solve. The moment you can meaningfully measure the value of buying from us against your business goals is when we will partner with you in that celebration."

Being an ASP means that you must also partner with your customers to help them measure the value of your offering, to quantify it so the customers can see the growth on their revenue, margins, and shareholder value. Your goal is for them to ultimately see your competitive differentiation so that you can partner with them and bring them insight on the next business problem or opportunity to solve, together.

So that's what I mean when I say, "the keys to the kingdom." The S-curve, which documents the customer-buying journey, can inform you, the ASP, exactly where you're entering into the customer's buying process. From that entry point, you can identify what activities are taking place and what you need to bring to the table.

For instance, if you didn't bring the **awareness** to the problem but are fortunate enough to enter the activity low and early, such as in the **investigation** phase, then the first thing you need to tell the customer is something along the lines of, "Help me understand the key business problem that this investigation is setting out to solve and who at the executive level owns that problem, because I want to partner with you to help them."

Or let's say you're entering low and late, for instance, in the **project** phase or the **evaluation** phase, which according to the

Corporate Executive Board (CEB) is roughly where a majority of first meaningful contacts between buyer and seller occur. According to CEB research in the book *The Challenger Sale*, most new opportunities for a sales rep entering into customers' sales activity pipeline happen when customers are 60 percent through their journey. They've already used online digital content to begin their buying journey before they first engage with a representative of a potential supplier or provider.[19] At Winning Adaptive Sales, we call this "vendor jail."

Yet when salespeople enter at that 60 percent point in the customer-buying journey S-curve, the first thing they start talking about is their own company—facts and figures about how great and stable they are, their product features and functions, and so on. They're a walking, talking version of their company's website or collaterals—stuff the buyer already knows. *I already know what you do and how you do it*, the buyer is thinking. *Tell me **why** you do it. Bring me some insight. Tell me what makes you different. Do you do this to be a partner to help us achieve our goals, or do you do this selfishly so that you can obtain your quota or your company's goals?*

If the S-curve is telling you that the three buying questions your customers are asking themselves are, in order, *Why change?*, *Why now?*, and *Why you?*, and your messaging is starting with "Why you?", then you're not aligned with the customer's buying journey.

You have to be able to answer the "Why change?" question first. You have to lead with, "This is what is driving organizations like yours to make changes. And by the way, I've got great experiences with those change initiatives based on my customer base. Let me bring you some insights around those business problems or opportu-

---

19 | Brent Adamson and Matthew Dixon, *The Challenger Sale: Taking Control of the Customer Conversation*, (New York: Penguin, 2011).

nities." You have to recast the problem so the customers start to see you as a long-term partner as opposed to a short-term vendor.

If you don't know the value or the impact on their strategic initiative, then you have to be able to create a hypothesis or a best estimate as to what the real impact could be on their competitive advantage, revenue growth needs, or margin growth requirements. Then, if they come at you with an opposing view, at least you've opened the conversation.

But if you don't ultimately have the "Why change?" and "Why now?" from their voice, then you will lose in negotiation, even if you win the deal. You'll be a supplier or a vendor that's selling a transaction almost on a commodity basis as opposed to being a partner helping them run their business more productively, more effectively, and more profitably.

MOMENTUM AND THE PIPELINE

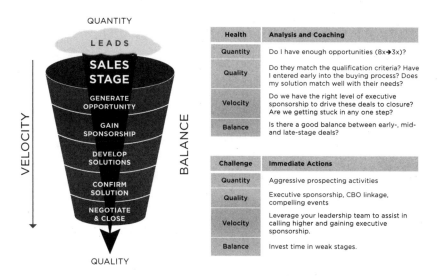

Health	Analysis and Coaching
Quantity	Do I have enough opportunities (8x→3x)?
Quality	Do they match the qualification criteria? Have I entered early into the buying process? Does my solution match well with their needs?
Velocity	Do we have the right level of executive sponsorship to drive these deals to closure? Are we getting stuck in any one step?
Balance	Is there a good balance between early-, mid- and late-stage deals?

Challenge	Immediate Actions
Quantity	Aggressive prospecting activities
Quality	Executive sponsorship, CBO linkage, compelling events
Velocity	Leverage your leadership team to assist in calling higher and gaining executive sponsorship.
Balance	Invest time in weak stages.

Having earned your place in the customer-buying journey, you must optimize the process by continually determining the health and welfare of your pipeline relative to the quality, quantity, velocity, and balance of your opportunities. Let me explain what I mean.

> **Quality.** The S-curve can help you identify how many quality opportunities you have to generate awareness of the business problem or opportunity, or to connect to the strategic initiative and the executive who owns it. Did you actually generate the awareness, or are you uniquely linked to the strategic initiative? Does the executive you've connected with own the strategy you're enabling, own or control the budget of the journey, or directly benefit from the results you will deliver? These are the kinds of questions you'll need to answer to determine the quality of your opportunities.

> **Quantity.** Quantity is the simplest piece of the pipeline to understand: How many opportunities do you have in process right now? Based on a salesperson's close rates, most complex-sales organizations want their salespeople to have three to eight times their quota in the pipeline to assure that they're going to hit their numbers. The quality of your connections can also affect quantity. For instance, the quality of your opportunities is higher if you are connected to a big strategic initiative because you're the one who generated awareness. When that happens, your quantity numbers tend to drop. And that's okay because having executive sponsorship on opportunities that solve big problems leads them to close faster and at a much higher amount.

> **Velocity.** You close deals faster when you are the salesperson who brings the awareness of a CBO at the top of the S-curve, the executive level. Executives who create the

strategy and have the authority to bind and commit the company's resources will accelerate (down the S-curve with sponsored momentum) all deals, big and small, if tied to achieving their strategic goals and CBOs.

Salespeople today labor under the impression that bigger deals take longer and are harder to close. It definitely feels that way when you enter low in the customer-buying process—if you enter into the process with management or staff—instead of high in the process with an executive sponsor. When you don't generate awareness at the executive level or you start low, in a valley of the process instead of at the peak, then you're left to climb onto the back of that manager or staff member and have him or her carry you up the hill to the executive team. That's a slow way to go.

Even when a sponsor refers you up to the leadership team, all of the executives' movements at the top of that hill then involve dislodging rocks and boulders—objections and challenges—that roll back down the S-curve hill, creating obstacles for you to overcome. Eventually, those objections are going to get too heavy and bothersome for the sponsor who's carrying you up the hill, unless you equip him or her with the tools needed to deal with those objections and accelerate up to the executives at the top. That's your goal: to get to the executives so that they can carry you through the S-curve of the customer-buying journey.

So momentum, or the "Law of Big Mo," matters in the S-curve. Where you enter—at the executive, management, or staff level—determines the momentum that you'll experience. If you enter down low, the velocity of your deal is going to be really slow. And frankly, the size of the deal will probably be smaller, because it didn't originate in the mind of the executive or the person who creates the higher-level strategies. If you start at the top and connect to something that's really big for the person, price is never an issue. That executive or leader will invest in what is required to accomplish the most important goals.

> **Balance.** When it comes to managing your pipeline, the bottom line is that you must have a good balance between early-, mid-, and late-stage deals. From targeting through selling and closing, you must have a good, healthy balance so you don't have big dry spells in your pipeline. You must aim for the deals that are high and early in the customer-buying journey, which garner the greatest momentum, but you must not pass on deals where you have no choice but to enter at the management and/or staff level—even though these management/staff-level deals are typically more transactional in nature and often described as mid- or late-stage sales opportunities. Now that you understand the customer-buying journey, you'll be able to bring insights and make the most of those deals, wherever your customer is in the process.

Again, entering in the middle or late in the customer-buying journey shouldn't hinder your efforts. Here's an example of how one of my business partners and I entered low and midway into a journey and yet were able to connect to the initiative and carry the executive's weight through the depths of the process. The executive then accelerated us to the closing and to an even larger deal than was originally anticipated.

The journey began at a father/son outing called Donuts with Dads at my son's school, Whitefield Academy, where I was fortunate to begin a long-standing friendship with the father of one of my son's schoolmates. One day, my friend approached me as I was dropping off my son at school, and he told me that the NASCAR team owner he worked for was looking for another corporate sponsor. The team owner had been approached by one of Mexico's wealthiest businessmen, who was looking for a way to improve the global perception of Mexicans through motorsports. One of the businessman's goals was to have a great Mexican athlete be recognized globally in his sport, and he saw NASCAR as that opportunity—in fact, he had a driver targeted who excelled in the NASCAR Mexico series.

At the time my friend approached me, the NASCAR team owner had been unable to locate a US-based corporation to sponsor the Mexican driver. Coincidentally, at that time, I had a client that was already involved in a customer relationship with the Mexican businessman's companies. In addition, my client had just acquired a new division of a well-known American telecommunications equipment manufacturer, and it needed some new brand recognition. Connecting dots, I thought that my client might be interested in using NASCAR as a way to gain greater recognition for its new acquisition as well as to change its global intimacy with one of its largest clients.

So my friend set up a meeting where my business partner and I met with the NASCAR team owner, who described to us the opportunity and challenge that he was faced with. We told the team owner about how our client might be a solution to his challenge, and we said we wanted to put together a plan to make that happen.

At first, the team owner opposed the idea—he wanted to begin making calls himself, in part because he saw the value in the idea but also because he wanted to get things moving rather quickly. He also wanted to sidestep what we saw as a need to build more trust with our client, largely because the deal was sizable compared to the client's annual marketing expenditure.

But the team owner's biggest concern was the experiences he'd had with sponsor development agents in the past; he told us that he'd signed agreements before but would then be left doing all the heavy lifting. In essence, he thought my partner and I were only trying to put together a deal to benefit our bottom line, and he was concerned that we would disappear after the fact without meaningfully participating and contributing to the effort required to close a deal of that magnitude.

But we didn't ask him—or anyone else involved in the deal—to sign a contract or make guarantees for our efforts in pursuit of the deal. Instead, we asked for the NASCAR team to consider working with us, after the fact, should we successfully bring a sponsor to the table. We told the team owner we were confident that we would be able to develop a good business relationship in the future, and he agreed.

After my partner and I met with our client stakeholders and had them on board with the idea, the team owner flew all of us to Mexico City to meet with the businessman and discuss the idea.

In the end, we were able to coordinate a three-year sponsorship deal that enabled one of Mexico's favorite drivers to be on the US NASCAR team and allowed the US NASCAR owner to add a fourth team to his roster. Our client sponsored the team, expanding its brand. And the Mexican businessman achieved his goal of having greater, positive exposure for one of his country's athletes.

Ultimately, it was a win all around, and my partner and I made it happen by being focused on the client's needs and wants instead of our own. And even though we came into the process low, we found a way to get on the decision maker's calendar and to use our momentum to carry him through the entire cycle—all in a 120-day time frame.

So quality, quantity, velocity, and balance help you identify the health of your pipeline. By using the customer-buying journey S-curve and staying others focused to identify where you need to correct or improve along the way, you can have a good, healthy balance as you lead customers through their buying journeys.

Now we've talked about the journey. So how do you engage executives so they will open their calendars to you and give you the audience to bring them real insight?

CHAPTER 5

ENGAGING EXECUTIVES—THE ONLY PROPOSAL THAT MATTERS

S olution selling is dead. That's essentially the declaration by *Harvard Business Review* (HBR) in its July-August 2012 issue.[20]

Back in 2011, when *The Challenger Sale* book containing the CEB's research first came out, it contained three tenets: customers are empowered now, they're out educating themselves, and what executive decision makers really want is to be taught something that they don't currently know and are not currently getting from their existing set of trusted advisors. That's what led HBR to report that "the celebrated 'solution sales rep' can be more of an annoyance than an asset."[21]

---

20 | Brent Adamson, Matthew Dixon, and Nicholas Toman, "The End of Solution Sales," *Harvard Business Review,* July-August 2012, 2016, https://hbr.org/2012/07/the-end-of-solution-sales.

21 | Ibid.

The CEB's research also found that executive decision makers want the insights they're getting from advisors outside their organizations to be tailored specifically to them and their CBOs, not just to them generally as a CEO or other C-level role. They want insights that are customized to what they need to know specifically as heads of their respective corporations.

That tailoring enables the executives to feel more in control of their destinies and the future of their organizations. As a selling professional, if you're going to engage executives in a way that they want to be engaged, then you must come to the table with an entirely new set of tools that have prepared you for that conversation. That begins by becoming the executives' trusted advisor.

People from all walks of life know who they consider to be their trusted advisors, both personally and professionally. For most people, it's a pretty small list—just look at your favorites list in your smartphone (compared to your entire list of contacts). Somewhere in that favorites list, there are a handful of people you would consider trustworthy enough to go to for advice. These are the people you feel you could be transparent with—they won't judge you, and they will be there to help guide you.

The idea of becoming a trusted advisor is daunting for the majority of salespeople out there. Most sales professionals selling complex goods and services are not confident enough to go in and meet with one of the top executives of their customers or prospects and have a strategic-business conversation. They're just not comfortable executing that conversation, because they're not conditioned for that executive engagement.

In part, it's because they simply don't have a base of knowledge of what is important to those executives. At the core, there really are only five key metrics that drive executives at the largest corporations of the world. As an ASP, these can help you lead a compelling executive conversation:

1. **Growing revenue.** Executives are concerned about growing the revenue of the company. The tactics that drive revenue could be the go-to-market strategy or the distribution model (i.e., direct sales versus channel sales), among other factors. But on the highest level, it's all about revenue growth.

   If you're going to engage an executive, then you must have an insightful, provocative, challenging statement of either a strong, fact-based opinion or consensus data that connects to the number-one goal of any executive— growing revenue.

2. **Controlling costs.** Executives are concerned about how to control costs, which is not always about spending less money. They just want to spend the right amount of money to grow the revenue at the best rate that they can so that they can accomplish another metric they're thinking about—profit or margin.

3. **Increasing profitability or margin.** If the executive is growing revenue and controlling costs, then there is going to be profit or margin in the business. Margin enables executives to better manage the next two metrics—market share and shareholder value.

4. **Improving market share.** One of the largest technology companies in the world is led by a man who has built up such an incredible wealth base that he owns 98 percent of Lanai, one of the Hawaiian Islands. Larry Ellison, executive chairman and chief technology officer of Oracle Corporation, clearly has business acumen and the ability

to execute. Ellison says market share is the number-one thing that executives care about; according to Ellison, market share isn't something—it's *everything*.

A company with a growing margin can decide how to use those dollars to expand its share of the market. A captive market enables executives who have the right focus to continue to invest, innovate, grow, and ultimately bring significance to customers and the market that the company serves.

5. **Increasing shareholder value.** The value of the business is a key metric for executives. For publicly traded companies, shareholder value drives the concept of market capitalization—basically the currency used to grow the business through acquisition, new product development, new market expansion, and so on.

As a sales professional, you must condition and prepare yourself to go into a meeting with a top executive of any company, no matter how large or small, and have a credible, strategic conversation that engages him or her around the five metrics that drive every executive.

Understanding these metrics and engaging the executive around them helps you quickly create an emotional and personal connection with that executive and set you on the path to becoming a trusted advisor.

These days, trust doesn't come from playing golf with clients or getting them into a special event; it comes from helping them accomplish one of their top CBOs. This is the opposite of the way selling used to be done. Sales professionals used to build personal relationships first and sell second. The shift in the market today, however, has executives asking up front for help in solving big problems or addressing opportunities in their business. Do that for an executive before you take them to their alma mater's basketball game—then you'll have the basis for becoming a trusted advisor.

DISCOVERING THE OBJECTIVES

So how do you become confident and conditioned to lead a strategic executive business conversation? In addition to having a high volume of quality inputs that teach you how to think and how to create a hypothesis around the CBOs of an executive, you must also discover and define just what those CBOs are. How you do that is a fairly simple but largely lost art.

The secret is this: a publicly traded company is required to report the risk factors facing the business to all shareholders to inform them of the risks associated with their investments in that business. Since the CEO and the board are obligated to publicly disclose that information and to let shareholders know what they're doing as a business plan to address those risks, you as a sales professional have immediate insight into the challenges or problems—the CBOs—that the executive team and the board of that organization are focused on addressing.

Even if you're selling to a privately held company, which doesn't have to publicly report its risk factors—only the private investors in that company have access to such information—you still have some level of insight into the organization. How? You can read about what's pressing down on the publicly traded companies in that industry. If you research a publicly traded company's 10-Q quarterly report, its 10-K annual report, or its letter to shareholders, you can familiarize yourself with the information and create a hypothesis from that research to use in engaging an executive at a privately held company.

The ability to then use what you find to deliver meaningful recommendations is a skill that is difficult to master and often taken for granted. Engaging executives is about getting on their level and doing so with confidence. What builds that confidence is conditioning—the amount of time you invest in preparation. Throughout Malcolm Gladwell's best-selling book *Outliers*, the author repeatedly mentions the "10,000 Hour Rule," claiming that the key to achieving world-class success in any skill is, to a large extent, a matter of practicing for around ten thousand hours. The ten thousand hours of exercise is the difference maker. That's what gave Bill Gates the confidence to leave college and build an empire that changed the world and launched him to the position of the wealthiest man in the world. Your hour-by-hour preparation—a.k.a. your conditioning—leading up to the ten thousand hours will build your confidence and help you execute.

Conditioning is the difference between DSRs and the associates and partners inside today's high-level business-strategy consulting firms—McKinsey & Company, Boston Consulting Group, Accenture, or Bain & Company. The way those associates and partners think and prepare is what enables them to confidently go in and bring insights, recommendations for growth, or problem resolutions to the large companies and executives that they engage with each day. You can read more about this in *The McKinsey Mind*, by Ethan Rasiel and Paul Friga. You can also read about how "McKinseyites" (as they call themselves) execute in *The McKinsey Way*, by Ethan Rasiel.

These books can really help differentiate you as an ASP. Tips in these publications can further help you engage executives around the things that matter to them in a way that is unique compared to other sources of advice that they're getting today. These tips can help you earn the opportunity to become one of the new advisors that your customers deem trustworthy. If you don't feel that you have the time to read these books, then getAbstract.com has five-page summaries for both *The McKinsey Mind* and *The McKinsey Way*.

WHAT? SO WHAT? NOW WHAT?

To ensure that your advice and insight hits the mark when you deliver it to your customer or prospect, employ what I call the "What? So What? Now What?" test.

Ask yourself these three questions regarding any advice or insight you intend to provide your customer:

> **What?** What key facts should be highlighted?

> **So What?** What is the impact (positive or negative) of those key facts on the customer and their business?

> **Now What?** What are the immediate priorities to recommend the customer take advantage of to remedy the situation?

If you have these answers, even if they are wrong in the eyes of the customer, customers will engage in a meaningful conversation about what is really driving their business and their decision-making priorities.

You must also be able to balance the continuum of sharing, asking, and listening to effectively sell using the insights you've discovered. All of us are somewhere on the journey from developing to mastering the art of sharing, bringing to the conversation an intriguing industry statistic or reference that provokes interest, demonstrates knowledge, and builds credibility.

Once you've shared, you must also have the confidence and competence to ask good questions that confirm the customer's understanding, gain alignment, and engage customers to share information about themselves, their businesses, and/or their challenges.

For example, in a conversation with a manufacturing prospect about how technology relates to momentum in the industry, you might ask questions such as these: What types of new technology are the company considering to improve customer spending and loyalty? What factors influence levels of automation in the company's plants? Do cloud solutions factor into any of the opportunities the company is considering?

Finally, you must also be a great listener. Don't stop after you've gone through all the work to gain and share insights and have asked thought-provoking questions. When asking questions, be confident and patient enough to truly listen to the customer's answers and use your critical-thinking skills to develop a sincere and authentic response. Remember, the less you say, the better you sound! If the customer is actively sharing, then you must actively listen.

ADAPTIVE SALES UNIVERSITY MEMBERSHIP

Engaging executives is about bringing real, tangible advice so that the executive can begin to trust and build their business plans around those insights. As a member of Adaptive Sales University, you'll get insights into the obstacles companies face in their industries. These can help you uniquely link your offerings to those obstacles and break them down so you can help your customers achieve their top objectives.

Adaptive Sales University can help you develop a hypothesis statement and learn how to deliver that message in a way that is credible, is passionate, and emotionally connects with your customer.

We also give you great conversation starters based on a client's objectives. We give you questions about the top data items pertaining to CBOs companies are focused on, helping you increase conditioning and find your voice.

USING TECHNOLOGY TO ENGAGE EXECUTIVES

To begin the process of engaging executives, start by reaching them where they are—social media. Technology is an ideal tool for connecting with executives and engaging them where they're looking for insights.

Begin on LinkedIn by considering your networking resources: Where are the executives you're trying to reach? How are your current relationships set up to get you referred to them? If you don't already have some networking avenues, then you'll need to set those up. Find out what events your executive targets are attending or where they're speaking. Get online and look for them on other social media platforms. What LinkedIn groups are they members of? Who are they following on Twitter? What are they tweeting? What are they posting? What are they blogging?

The information that you gather is then used as a basis for how to initiate direct contact either by phone, through e-mail, or in person. For example, if you have existing relationships from LinkedIn, get your network to lend credibility to your introduction. If you don't have those relationships, then use what you learned about the executive on LinkedIn and Twitter—what are they currently saying on social media? Use that knowledge to inform your e-mail headline, voicemail message, or introductory statement when you talk to the executive in person. And if you're one of the salespeople behind the statistic that only three out of every hundred cold calls connect (a 97 percent failure rate), but you want to up your numbers, then consider reading up on how to eliminate rejections in Art Sobczak's book, *Smart Calling*. Yes, there is a getAbstract for this book as well!

Finally, you must inform the executive by marketing yourself at a high level. Start by using social-selling tools to publish insights; publish on LinkedIn, write blogs, contribute to online publications, and create tweets and other content that will get executives to follow you. Get yourself out there as an authority by sharing ideas and insights that are free for them to consume. Then, when they consume your insights, you'll have a touchpoint for connecting with them.

If you want someone to view you as an advisor, someone who brings an authoritative point of view and voice to the table, then consider other avenues as well, such as websites and e-mail marketing through services like MailChimp or Constant Contact, speaking at conferences, and having a booth at trade shows where you talk about your perspectives.

It bears repeating: information and knowledge are not power—how you use information and knowledge determines what power you have in all sales activity. With over two billion smart devices on networks around the world today and more than three million app users consuming information on those devices in real time, at least a third of the world's population right now has access to the same information and knowledge.

That makes information and knowledge commodities—that's not real power. What's powerful is the way you execute with insight. Being an ASP is not about being a provider of information; executives have all the information they need at their fingertips. What they want is your thinking, your point of view, your interpretation, and recommendation as to what they should do with that information. If you are the one who says it first, if you say it in a way that resonates with their personality and connects with their business objective, and if they see you as a trustworthy resource, that's where the power of execution comes in. And that comes from finding your voice.

CHAPTER 6

EVERY CONVERSATION IS A STRATEGIC-BUSINESS CONVERSATION

B y now you can see the value of creating demand by being the source of awareness in the customer's buying journey, and that comes from calling high and early. This allows you to generate opportunities and be a part of the early momentum that comes with executive sponsorship. But while high and early is the ideal place to enter into the customer's buying cycle, there are *challenges*, *benefits*, and *risks* in early executive engagement.

The primary *challenge* of early executive engagement is just getting on the calendar—getting access by bringing something of value that makes the customer want to open up and give you time. The *benefit* of engaging early, and in the right way, is that it can get you that executive sponsorship quick, and you can use that momentum throughout the buying process. The *risk* is that if you don't have a compelling, strategic-business conversation with the executive, you will never get another chance. You have one opportunity to hit the target—that's it.

The *risk* piece is why many (if not most) sales professionals today will not go out of their comfort zone to go have those strategic-business conversations early with a targeted executive sponsor. They'll forgo that risk for the comfort zone of calling lower in the organization, at the manager level or even down at the staff level.

Still, there's also challenge, benefit, and risk with going in at that level, which I categorize as low level instead of executive level. The *challenge* with going in low is being able to empower and enable that lower-level person to take you back up to the executive level, where strategy and decisions are made. You can spend a lot of your time informing and educating staff and managers who aren't connected to the strategy that's driving the business. The *benefit* of coming in low is that you can usually get those meetings scheduled, and you can become a confidant of many people down lower in the organization. Through those meetings, you can form alliances that may ultimately open doors higher up—a slow-going avenue, but a road in nevertheless.

The *risk*, of course, is the time you may waste spinning your wheels. You may be educating people who have no pain in the business, no power to drive buying decisions. You're potentially depending on someone who is completely uninformed, and you're hoping that he or she is a self-starter who will take the initiative to make the connection up to the executive level. That's a huge risk.

So how do you rise up out of your comfort zone and into the power zone? How do you sell above the power line, that high-and-early space where the executives who drive the strategy and determine buy-in live? The only way that you make that happen is with a strategic-business conversation.

Regardless of who you're talking to in an organization, every conversation you have with your customers must be strategic. It must include insights and information that they aren't aware of inside or even outside their industry. Even if you've entered low, you must link your conversation strategically to the business goals and drivers that exist above the customers.

If you've seen the movie *Wall Street*, then you may have an idea of how difficult it can be to get the initial meeting with the top executive, and you can envision the challenge of bringing insight to the table (although I don't propose doing what the character Bud Fox did). In the movie, Michael Douglas plays a Wall Street powerhouse trader, Gordon Gekko, and Charlie Sheen plays wannabe Bud Fox. Everybody wants to be involved with Gekko because whatever his teams are involved in turn to gold; everyone wants to be able to bring Gekko insights that he will turn into off-the-chart investments.

In order for Bud Fox to get a meeting with Gekko—a nearly impossible task—Fox had to be persistent and get through Gekko's executive assistant. Failing dozens of times, Fox finds out when Gekko's birthday is and he shows up at Gekko's office with a box of the trader's favorite cigars. Finally granted "five minutes" with the trader, the tip Fox had to share was "a dog," according to Gekko, who already knew about and rejected the stock. Fox offers a second tip, which Gekko calls "a dog with different fleas." "Tell me something I don't know," Gekko says to Fox. Finally, Fox tosses out a tip that is ultimately insider trading—again, I'm not proposing that you do something unethical; "greed is not good" is my own spin on Gekko's oft-used phrase from the movie. The teaching point here is that you have to not only be persistent in *your call-high-early* efforts but also bring *something they don't already know* to engage in a *strategic-business conversation.* Otherwise, you are a *thief of their time*, and time is the one thing they can never get back![22]

Technology has changed the landscape when it comes to getting in doors. With executives having more access to information than ever, getting in the door with relevant insights to have a strategic-business conversation is tougher than ever—but it's not impossible! That's what Winning Adaptive Sales and our Adaptive Sales University is all about. You also have access to a wealth of information to use in forming hypotheses and creating strategic conversations. And you must use everything in your power to make the connection happen—as long as your tactics aren't unethical, immoral, or illegal, of course!

The pressure on sales professionals today is stronger than ever. That's why you have to invest in and use the data and resources at your disposal, and you must apply your critical-thinking skills to come up with something that is truly a differentiator. The key word I use here is you. Not your manager, not your company's marketing, product development, or product marketing departments—you. No features, functions, benefits, technical superiority, blanket marketing-developed messages, or presentations up front. Your insights must connect to one of the only five areas that mean anything to executives: growing revenue, controlling costs, increasing profitability or margin, improving market share, and increasing shareholder value.

There are thousands of tactics you can use to develop insights.

> ➤ **Current market research.** Look at the industry, the market, the specific business, the executive, and the stakeholders. What current trends are affecting a company's ability to execute in its operational performance? What's on

---

22 | Oliver Stone and Stanley Weiser, Wall Street, directed by Oliver Stone, film (1987).

the horizon that may affect the company—positively or negatively?

> **Critical thinking.** Look below the surface of an issue to make your hypothesis. What's entering the marketplace today in another industry that's going to affect your customer tomorrow?

> **Point of view.** If you're having trouble coming up with a solid point of view on an issue, read what other thought leaders are saying, and see whose comments make sense. Have passion and conviction about what path is best for your customer, and then find whose ideas best align with your customer's position.

> **Collaboration.** Look to others on your team or other industry leaders to bring insights to your customers. Be intentional in your discovery process with everyone you think may have something to contribute to your customer's success and ability to execute.

> **Observation.** Open your eyes to other industries, markets, regions, countries, and figures of authority for input and perspective. What have they said on record? What successes are they experiencing, and why? What missteps did they make that you can avoid? What adjustments are they making for corrective action, and to what effect?

> **Reflection.** Have you seen this issue in some other form before? Even events from our personal lives teach us things that can apply to business. Think about what you've done, what you've heard, and what you've witnessed in others, and use those lessons to help inform your customer. Use them as "talk tracks" for conversation (dialogue), not presentation (monologue).

> **Leverage.** Use what you've learned to make a difference—a difference that your customer would proactively share with others about your leadership in his or her accelerated success. You know you have achieved "T-R-U-S-T" with your customer when you receive a LinkedIn notice that he or she has written a recommendation about your work. What someone else says about you speaks volumes more than what you say about yourself!

Terminology is also key to demonstrating to your customer the value you bring. If you're calling on a general manager of an automobile dealership, and you're not using terms like "profit PNVR" (profit per new vehicle retailed), then you're not speaking their language. You'll be viewed as an outsider, and you'll be treated like one. And you can't just know what PNVR stands for; you have to know that, based on last year's NADA (National Automobile Dealers Association) studies, for the average automotive dealer in the United States, the PNVR is right at $1,000, whereas the average sales price for a new car is $30,000. Your critical-thinking skills have to tell you that those two numbers add up to a low-margin, high-volume business. Every value-oriented message you deliver to that target needs to connect with that business condition.

You also need to know regulatory trends. If you're calling on a financial institution, whether it's a Tier 1, Tier 2, or Tier 3 financial institution, you have to know how the Dodd-Frank Act is pressing down on the institution from an operational perspective. And if that financial institution is a credit union and you use the term "customer" instead of "member," they are going to know that you are one of the 45 percent of the salespeople in the market today who don't know the credit-union industry. Good luck with that deal being anything other than transactional and discount driven!

When you go in and talk to a managing partner at a law firm, your strategic-business conversation had better demonstrate that you know a thing or two about legal outsourcing and work-life balance. You should also understand details such as how, in order for the firm to build a winning court case, to best store electronic information that allows the firm to mine text messages, digital voicemail, and e-mails and securely store that information in a way that doesn't breach any confidentialities or security requirements.

If you're calling on physicians, you have to understand the deeper pain that the Affordable Care Act is inflicting on their ability to practice, and you have to have a strategic-business conversation about how you can help them not just survive but thrive. If you're calling on a clerical person in the practice, they're likely not feeling pain as acutely as the managing physicians. This is a perfect example of what it means to link your conversation to what matters to the decision makers. You'll get credit for giving them a value proposition to solve their immediate, day-to-day needs while also giving them a valuable conversation to have with their boss that raises their literacy and acumen. Remember that rising water lifts all boats. You must be the voice that helps everyone in your customer's organization *raise their game.*

By finding your voice and helping your customers find theirs, you'll be living Covey's "8th Habit." You'll be a FOLO leader; you'll become an accelerator of your customers' success by helping them be the water that lifts the company up and delivers what's important to the executives above them.

SELLING "5 O"

In order to have an effective business conversation, you need to have a consistent framework that enables you regardless of what kind of business executive you're calling on. This framework promotes conversation and dialogue—it's not a presentation that puts you in a box and places customers in a trap. It's a dynamic, flexible framework that encourages interaction between you (the ASP) and your customer.

That framework is a strategic-business conversation that we call the "5 Os."

Observations. The first *O* is your observations of what is happening in the executive's industry and how those trends are affecting them. You must begin by talking about *your* observations—not your *company's* observations—of what's going on in their industry. You must be the T-R-U-S-T-ed source.

The first *O* allows for you to be in the top 55 percent of all sales professionals calling on executives today: one of the 55 percent that knows the industry. And you'll not just know the current industry trends; you'll have an opinion of the impact on the executive's business that will lead you to potentially have a higher-level connection with that executive.

Objectives. What are the key objectives, the second *O*, that the executive is focused on achieving in his or her organization? Every executive and every owner is different based on the function that he or she performs, whether that leader is a chief executive, financial, operations, information, technology, marketing, or revenue officer.

Whatever their chief role, each of these leaders has a different set of objectives.

While we can slice and dice these objectives into specifics for the individual roles, for the purposes of discussion here, we'll lump them all into the top objectives of the "CXO," with "X" being any of the "chief" roles. So what are the top objectives that a CXO is out to accomplish in his or her business every single day?

> Grow top-line revenue.
> Reduce operating costs.
> Increase profitability or margin.
> Assure competitive differentiation or advantage.
> Parlay the aforementioned four objectives into an increasing shareholder value number.
> Reduce risk exposure of the company and its operations.
> Improve business reputation and consumer perception (e.g., sustainability, green initiatives, supporting the local community, etc.).

Having a knowledge base of these objectives can give you a starting point in a conversation. For instance, you might begin with, "As I've worked with other executives in your exact role in this industry, here are the things that I've seen them focus on to achieve the most on behalf of their shareholders." This is your G-2-G piece—you've worked with other executives to accomplish objectives, which are influenced and driven by what you've observed as going on in their industries.

Now, talking about objectives isn't just about asking open-ended questions. It's about getting to the heart of the obstacle that is preventing an executive from hitting his or her objectives. Here are a few more sample conversation starters—discovery questions that will get the executive talking:

> When you last did your strategic planning, what were the top two or three objectives that you were committed to that you thought were going to have the biggest impact on your business? And how are you doing toward achieving those?

> What key initiatives are you focused on to either reduce cost or increase profitability? What challenges do you anticipate or are you currently experiencing while working on these initiatives?

> What emerging technologies are your employees, customers, or partners asking for?

> What challenges are you facing to keep current customers (competition, price compression, service, etc.)?

Obstacles. This third *O* is about what's standing in the way of CXOs like the executives you're talking to; what's keeping them from hitting their objective? By having a confident statement about current obstacles and then asking key questions, you'll get the executive talking: "What are the obstacles that you're facing right now? What challenges are keeping you from hitting your objectives?" These kinds of targeted questions work over "What's keeping you up at night?", especially if you give them a little bit of your insight as to the obstacles that you're seeing affect other executives like them in their industry.

Here are some of the challenges standing in the way of CXOs hitting their objectives:

> operational inefficiency

> available cash flow

> resource productivity

> regulatory or compliance issues

> employee or customer churn (turnover or loss)

> lack of insight into technology expenses and the quantifiable impact on the business, especially social media

> maintaining the status quo because the pain of change is
> seen as being far greater than the pain of staying the same

The last of these obstacles or challenges—the "if it's not broken, don't fix it" mind-set—can paralyze or even kill a business because the race that used to be won by the biggest companies in the world is now being won by the fastest.

These days, people say, "No one gets fired for buying Cisco," because Cisco has become kind of a staple, if you will. That same thing used to be said years ago about IBM—but IBM was so big that it lost the speed of its innovation and reinvention capabilities. It lost the ability to stay connected with and relevant to customers. The company was standing on product sales as its platform—it had always had the best technology hardware in the world. But product selling and product differentiation gave way to using those products as tools or solutions to help customers solve business problems. Because IBM stayed so focused on product differentiation, it didn't think about solutions, insights, services, and the people that it takes to make those things happen. The company started to lose its way, and ultimately it reached the point where it had to sell high-value assets to other companies to prop up the rest of the business.

The CEO, Lou Gerstner, had to step in, assess the problem, and make huge course redirections—a hard reboot of the company. That's when IBM started building the business around the services, the thought leadership, and the people who use the hardware and give counsel and coaching to enable customers to grow. Today, IBM's Watson delivers insight to all forms of businesses. By the way, you can read about Gerstner's turnaround in his book, *Who Says Elephants Can't Dance?*, which documents how the IBM status quo nearly got the best of the company and its shareholders.

The race that is now being won by the fastest can't be done at reckless speed. It has to be a measured and targeted speed. The biggest companies that have speed, like Google, Apple, and Samsung, also have size—but speed is the differentiator.

Obstacles today are perilous for CXOs; they absolutely hinder CXOs from hitting their objectives.

Offerings. Only after you've addressed the first three *Os*—observations, objectives, and obstacles—do you come in with the fourth *O*—offerings. But offerings is still not about products, features, and functions—not just yet. You can back up your offerings with features and functions, but first and foremost, this *O* is about what your company brings to the table that breaks down obstacles and helps executives achieve their objectives based on your observations of what's going on in their industry.

Think about that. *You're synergizing your offerings as a way to break down obstacles and enable them to achieve their objectives based on the observations of what's really going on in their industry.*

> Synergize your offerings as a way to break down obstacles and enable them to achieve their objectives based on the observations of what's really going on in their industry.

Outcomes. The final *O* is about bringing in a story of outcomes—successes where you've helped other executives and companies achieve their objectives and breaking down their obstacles through your offerings. The best part is that you only need one great outcome story.

These 5 Os comprise a strategic-business conversation, and it's what your customers—especially executives—are craving. As much as possible, create the framework for a conversation—not a presentation—around the 5 Os: *observations* of the industry, *objectives* of the executives, *obstacles* that they're facing daily, *offerings* you have that can break those obstacles down to help them achieve their objectives, and *outcomes* that you've experienced with other companies like theirs.

The 5-Os framework can be the difference maker for you being seen as an advisor—as an insight provider. It can help you have the "Law of Big Mo" on your side.

Let me give you an example of a 5-Os conversation I had earlier in my career. When I was working as a senior account executive for a major ERP software company in the mid-1990s, one of my prospects was a market leader in the vertical transportation business (elevators). This was before the Internet, and I was just coming off the incident where I had been publicly humbled by my manager. In the aftermath of that public shaming, I built entire dossiers on all my targets.

I had been trying to get a meeting with the elevator company for about a year, with no real success, when one day the phone rang— it was the CIO of the company. Because I had been preparing, I knew who he was, which took him by surprise very early in the conversation.

He told me that the company had a big project underway, and he wanted me to fly down and talk to the group as part of the evaluation process. He wanted me to look things over and then propose products and services for the company's ERP solution needs. He asked me to come as soon as possible.

While obviously we wanted to work with the company, instead of leaping at the chance to take him up on his offer and talk in-depth about products and solutions, I launched into an insightful strategic-business conversation with him about my observations.

I told him that I understood who his competition was and what his company was likely challenged with. "You're struggling with going from sales-opportunity pursuit all the way into a certified vertical transportation system on-site as fast as or faster than the top three competitors you're working with," I hypothesized. He confirmed that I was right.

I told him that those other companies were also our customers, so I had some insight into what they were doing. Then I began asking him questions and getting confirmation on some numbers involved in the potential deal: how many end users, what kind of hardware and software was involved, and what kinds of fees he was looking at. I basically laid out the entire project at his feet, including insights about the scope of the project that he hadn't yet considered—other likely vendors, professional staff and services, additional hardware that would be needed, and other budget factors.

Finally, I told him, "We want to get engaged. We know your industry intimately. And we've got some unique insights that can help you really compete even better around how to organize your business processes inside the latest and greatest client/server solution. But you're going to have to get your CFO on the line and your board in agreement, because this is a $100 million investment. We're going to need to know that they can get that type of appropriation before I will be able to fly down and help you in this process."

After a few minutes of silence on his end, he came back with, "You mean I have to get my CFO to go to the board and get a preliminary commitment on the funds before you'll even come talk to me?"

"Yes," I confirmed. It's a more efficient way of approaching the opportunity for both of us, I told him. "Once we have that, I will unleash all of the resources of the company I work for. We will be at your disposal to make sure that you have everything you need to make an informed decision so you can't just compete, but you can thrive over your competition. We'd love to help you do that."

My approach was the opposite of the other two major vendors the client was working with. In that conversation, he knew that I understood his industry because I was speaking his vernacular—"vertical transportation," not "elevators." I knew who the company's competitors were, and I knew what it took to go from a construction-site bid all the way to getting an elevator certified for passenger transport by the local authorities. I knew the objectives of the company's executive team and its board. I knew the obstacles that the company would run into as relating to hardware, software, people, databases, financials, and so on. I had positive outcomes that I could reference. Plus, I used the 5-Os conversation to demonstrate my knowledge. At that point, he began to see me as an authority in his industry.

Two weeks later, I got a call from the CFO. He had met with the board and received acknowledgment and approval that the funds would be available should my company be the winning bidder.

Competing hard, six months later, we landed that piece of business.

The 5-Os framework works, and we've continued to adapt the 5-Os framework based on the current changing conditions of today's more empowered buyer.

MY "STORY-SELLING" STYLE

In order for you to be able to execute really well with the 5 Os, you must also develop a very sincere and authentic communication style—a storytelling style that sells—something I call "My Story

Selling!" . . . Because you're not going to sell to today's executives based solely on facts, figures, and data.

Facts, figures, and data support emotion, and the 5-Os framework is a way to create an emotionally connected conversation with executives around the strategic-business initiative or business objective.

Still, your story must be mapped to the individual personality of the buyer or executive you're talking to because everyone's personality is unique, and the way we communicate actually matters more than what we communicate. What's the best method for doing that?

The Birkman Method is a scientifically developed personality assessment for improving people skills and aligning roles and relationships for maximum productivity and success. The Birkman Method enables the ASP to better understand your own personality and communication style, and it can help you gauge who you believe your customer or prospect is from a personality-style perspective.

By using the Birkman Method to understand your own personality and gauge your buyers', you'll be able to adapt your communication style to theirs in the way that they need to be communicated with for the best possible outcome. It will allow you to follow a framework for a strategic-business conversation, regardless of who you're working with or calling on.

The Birkman Method lets you know your usual communication or personality style as a sales professional. For instance, are you a talker? If so, then you're a direct communicator and are very people oriented. The Birkman Method categorizes that style as "green." Are you a doer, meaning you're a direct communicator but are task oriented? Doers are categorized as "red." If you're an administrator or a counter, then you're an indirect communicator and are task oriented. You are categorized as "yellow." Or if you are a thinker, then you're an indirect communicator and are people oriented and categorized as "blue."

Knowing your style and quadrant color matters because everyone that you'll call on and have meetings with will also have a personality style that falls inside of one of the four color quadrants defined by the Birkman Method.

If, for example, you're a green talker—people oriented and a direct communicator—and the person you're meeting with is green as well, then there's a high likelihood that the two of you will connect around your executive, 5-Os-based conversation.

If, however, you're a green and the person you're meeting with is a yellow—an indirect communicator who is task oriented—then you need to know that right away. Yellow personalities tend to be much more process-oriented, risk-averse, and data-driven decision makers. They take their time and are very deliberate, objective, and logical. Green personalities tend to be more big-picture oriented, rapid, and spontaneous.

Why is it important to understand the style of the person you're communicating with? Because even if you say the right message to the right person at the right time around the right problem, you will lose the deal if you do it in the wrong personality style.

Imagine that. You've identified the right business problem of the right person at the right time, but you deliver it in the wrong way—and you lose. That's why it's critical to have a strategic-business conversation in a way that will connect to how your prospect or customer needs to be communicated with.

Since the Birkman Method helps you read somebody's personality style, body language, tone of voice, method of talking, orientation to time, and orientation to others, it can help you recognize and adapt to changes throughout a conversation. By observing people's facial expressions and tone of voice, you can understand their personality at any given moment in time. That will allow you to adapt your personality style and communication to theirs.

In my career, I have been exposed to training claiming that personal communication is 7 percent the words a person says, 38 percent tone of voice, and 55 percent body language. Accepting those figures as accurate, if a lot of your selling is done by phone, then you're going to miss over half of what your customer is really communicating because you can't see his or her body language. With the proliferation of video conferencing on ultra-high-speed networks, I recommend using video calls over voice calls as often as possible to avoid missing 55 percent of your target's communication style.

The Birkman Method has been used for personality assessment for more than sixty years; nearly fifty million personality reports have been run using the Birkman Method. Birkman claims to be (and I believe to be true) the only personality tool that identifies the underlying motivators that drive someone's personality—interests, usual behaviors, underlying needs, stress behaviors, and more.[23]

How valuable would it be for you if you knew the unspoken motivators that were driving the personality behaviors of the individual stakeholder you were working with? If you knew that, just like if you knew where the customer was in the buying process, you would absolutely have an advantage over your competition. You would have the ability to connect in a meaningful, insightful, adaptive way that would set you apart in the eyes of your customer.

By knowing your own personality style, you can adapt and map—not mirror—your delivery to each individual buyer. And by understanding your own communication style, you can respond in a way that creates a smooth, comfort-oriented conversation. You can

23 | Birkman International, https://birkman.com/.

adapt your behavior, your language, and the content of your message to sincerely connect with the buyer.

CHAPTER 7

FIND YOUR VOICE

I f every conversation you're having with a customer or prospect is a strategic-business conversation, you have to adapt that strategic-business conversation to the personality style of the individual. You must also understand that an individual personality can change based on a person's current mood or feeling. So it's critical that you adapt to a customer's in-the-moment personality style and help that person find his or her voice around the insight you're bringing to the table.

That comes down to finding your voice. The *difference makers (a.k.a. Trident Carriers)* are those sales professionals who find their voice in helping others find theirs. That's when you go from being an effective salesperson to being a great ASP—a "T-R-U-S-T-ed" advisor.

Finding your voice starts with your attitude. The way you feel inside inspires what comes out of you—your voice, your energy, your body language. All of those pieces of personal communication are observed and perceived as worthy of connection from the person on the other side of the conversation.

The tools I've shared with you enable you, as an Adaptive Sales Professional, to be an artist—to create something insightful and innovative, because it's the skill of the craftsman that makes the difference in the outcomes. It would be like giving two woodworkers the same tool and the same raw material—a chainsaw and an eight-foot-long oak log, two feet in diameter, for example—to see what they produce. One of those woodworkers might use the saw to cut the log into two-foot lengths to be split into firewood and sold in the open market for $200. Someone who is adaptive, innovative, and insightful might see more than a fuel source in that same log; they might see a bear or tiger or another creative figure dying to be released from its current trap, ultimately to be sold in the open market for $2,000: same tools, same raw materials, ten times more value. The difference is the insight and skill of the adaptive woodworker.

The way to develop creativity and innovative skill is through continuous coaching and mentoring by someone who has more experience and knows how to use his or her voice in a way that helps you find yours. A leader or mentor can help you have a voice that helps other people see the beauty in a situation; a voice that helps them hear and understand the insights and advice that you are sharing; a voice that helps others envision opportunities for growth.

At WinningAdaptiveSales.com, our why—our drive—is to connect insights and tools to sales professionals looking to become artisans. We want you to be able to connect with the best teachings, techniques, tools, and leaders in the industry—leaders who will work with you in one-on-one sessions or in small or large groups.

We want to help you find your voice so that you can be the artisan of sales who brings out the best in customers. We want you to be appreciated for the art form you're bringing to the table, for the masterful way in which you help your clients grow their business based on the rapidly changing environment that they live in.

It takes continual pursuit to adapt who you are today to who you really want and need to be tomorrow. That's what finding your voice is all about.

BREAKING THROUGH THE BRAIN BARRIERS OF CHANGE

In reading this book, I hope that either you are or you may become engaged in a significant transformation.

In their book, *Leading Strategic Change: Breaking Through the Brain Barrier*, J. Stewart Black and Hal Gregersen wrote that if a strategic change is what you desire in life, then you're going to run into three brain barriers.

The first brain barrier is that you must first see the need to change. Data shows that if you are not adapting based on the current changing environments of complex sales, you will either become a DSR, or you're already dying and you just don't know it. I hope this book has made you see the need to change.

Brain barrier number two is taking that first step, which is counterintuitive to the way almost all sales organizations and salespeople sell today—they sell what they do and how they do it because they believe that leads to a logical buying decision. It doesn't. It may support how a decision is made, but it doesn't drive why decisions are made—which is always based on personal, human emotion. In this book, I've given you some of the first steps to take and assembled a wealth of resources to help in that effort.

The third brain barrier is figuring out how to make the change toward your new habit—your new norm. WinningAdaptiveSales. com and Adaptive Sales University are the places where great content and a network of willing and able leaders will help you go from taking the first step to creating new habits. If you're ready, let's get started. We're going to help you break through the three brain barriers to strategic change and watch you grow to become a member of the top 1 percent of all complex salespeople—a Trident Carrier.

Whether you are new to the profession of sales and are hungry to adapt to the latest and best practices, or you are a seasoned veteran who has been in sales for decades and feels like there's nothing left to learn, I want to bring you new insights that can take you from where you are right now to that degree of success that you so desire.

Still need convincing? Look at it this way: What happens when water reaches 211 degrees Fahrenheit? If you think the answer is that the water boils, you're wrong. At 211 degrees, water is just really hot. At 212 degrees, it boils. With boiling water comes steam. From steam you can generate power to run locomotives, light cities, and more.

That one degree of growth is what makes the difference between having really hot water and having the power to be the best that you can be.

ADAPTIVE SALES UNIVERSITY

Membership in Winning Adaptive Sales includes access to Adaptive Sales University, where you will find the leaders, insights, and tools to enable you to be in the top 1 percent of ASPs—a Trident Carrier!

These resources are designed to help you find your voice and build sustainable T-R-U-S-T with your customers. They are customizable to you and your situation to help you synergize with your prospects. Using these tools will not just take you from where you are to where you want to be but will also continue to help you adapt to market and industry changes, which will continue to happen at warp speed.

Our insights, tools, and leadership are always adapting to help you gain the best leverage based on your goals, desires, and personality. Our leaders live and breathe the core values and principles of Winning Adaptive Sales—the number-one principle, of course, is being others focused.

We want to come alongside and lead you to your highest level of desired growth.

We would be honored to have you as a member for the long term and to share the impact of your membership with others around you who could benefit from staying ahead of the game in the rapidly changing world of complex sales.

Adaptive Sales University modules address sales and service, leadership and management, and personal development. Throughout the three modules are over eighty courses with high-value outcomes to support the principles of Winning Adaptive Sales.

For instance, in the sales and service module, areas of study range from selling techniques to communication skills to negotiation strategies—everything you need to be the most effective ASP you can be. In the leadership and management module, you learn about effective time- and task-managing skills, forecasting models, understanding costs and preparing budgets, dealing with people, and a full complement of studies designed to help you be a FOLO leader. And in the personal-development module, areas of study include understanding different personality types, influencing strategies, problem solving using creative and methodical methods, and more.

Annual membership to Adaptive Sales University includes unlimited access to course content to a network of leaders and members for networking and peer-level professional development.

Adaptive Sales University is the only platform that bridges capabilities of Facebook, LinkedIn, SlideShare, and Khan Academy for corporate education, specifically for sales, leadership, and personal skill advancement.

Adapting is all about advancing based on your current environment and surroundings. Those current environment and surroundings change daily. Winning Adaptive Sales is about equipping you not just with the tools you need but also with the know-how to use the tools for your advancement. Remember: the tool itself is only as effective as the skill of the person using it. But with the right leadership and coaching, you will become an absolute artisan at Winning Adaptive Sales. You will avoid becoming a DSR. You will instead be encouraged, equipped, and enabled to live a "Yes You Can" life!